Vision

TO M. L. A.

VISION

Variations on Some Berkeleian Themes

Robert Schwartz

BLACKWELL
Oxford UK & Cambridge USA

First published 1994

Blackwell Publishers
238 Main Street
Cambridge, Massachusetts 02142
USA

108 Cowley Road
Oxford OX4 1JF
UK

Library of Congress Cataloging-in-Publication Data

Schwartz, Robert, 1940–
     Vision : variations on some Berkeleian themes / Robert Schwartz.
          p. cm.
     Includes bibliographical references and index.
     ISBN 1–55786–220–6 (alk. paper) – ISBN 1–55786–536–1 (pbk. alk. paper)
     1. Berkeley, George, 1685–1753. Essay towards a new theory of
vision.   2. Vision—Research.   3. Philosophy of mind.   I. Title.
B1339.S38   1994
121'.3—dc20   93–19417
                                                                                                      CIP

British Library Cataloguing in Publication Data

A CIP catalogue record for this book is available from the British Library.

Typeset in 11 on 13 pt Garamond
by Graphicraft Typesetters Ltd., Hong Kong

This book is printed on acid-free paper

CONTENTS

Preface

For a good number of years, I have offered a course on historical and contemporary theories of vision. I have always started with a thorough reading of George Berkeley's *An Essay Towards a New Theory of Vision*, with the aim of acquainting students with Berkeley's important contributions to developments in the theory of vision, rather than pondering the possible metaphysical and epistemological implications of his ideas. In the second half of the course, I look at how various of the problems Berkeley considers are addressed in subsequent empirical work on vision. What, for example, does current visual theory tell us about the nature of distance perception, size perception and the moon illusion, the problem of the inverted retinal image, the relationship between sight and touch, the question of learning versus innateness, and the role of inference in vision?

Invitations to speak at sundry universities and conferences led me to put some of this course material into the form of papers. I had originally intended to publish several of these as separate articles, but Stephan Chambers at Blackwells convinced me that there was enough cohesion among the essays to publish them as a book.

I wish to thank the many friends, colleagues, and students who have heard and commented on earlier versions of this material. I also wish to thank Nelson Goodman for introducing me to the splendors of Berkeley's writings on vision. I have benefited from discussing my ideas with Carl Zuckerman, Sidney Morgenbesser, and, most especially, Margaret Atherton. My thoughts about Berkeley have coalesced with hers so much that I frequently find it difficult to separate her contributions from my own. In her book *Berkeley's Revolution in Vision*, she reported on some of the results of our discussions and on some ideas found in a circulated but unpublished paper of mine, "Seeing Distance from a Berkeleian Perspective." I expand on this material in the present essays.

I have tried to cite psychological works that are reasonably available and accessible to the nonexpert. As a result, my references are not always to the very latest or most technically sophisticated presentation of the position mentioned. Illustrations were prepared by Mary Gainer. My work on this book was supported by NSF grant no. SES 8408686 and by a summer grant from the University of Wisconsin – Milwaukee.

Introduction

This book consists of four related essays examining some longstanding problems in the theory of vision. Each of the essays begins by looking at the issues as they are raised and discussed in George Berkeley's classic *An Essay Towards a New Theory of Vision*.[1] Berkeley's formulations and solutions are explored. But clarifying the work of Berkeley and other early researchers serves as a point of departure. Based on this historical background, along with analyses of current psychological research in the theory of vision, new approaches and solutions to these problems are considered.

Chapter 1 is the most historical, tracing the implications of Berkeley's views on distance perception for our understanding of such questions as: What does it mean to see distance? Is distance a property of the visual field? Can we see distance immediately? In the course of this discussion, special attention is paid to the significance of the discovery of the stereoscope and to the importance of movement in calibrating vision.

Chapter 2 focuses on the nature of size perception. Perhaps the most widely held theory of size perception has been the taking-account-of-distance model. In his *New Theory*, Berkeley argues against early versions of this model. Chapter 2 examines the geometric assumptions that underpin most old and new versions of the taking-account-of-distance approach. It is argued that when the consequences of these assumptions are made explicit, the model is rendered quite problematic.

Chapter 3 is concerned with the claim that processes of (unconscious) inference play a role in perception. This thesis, although widely promoted, has been subject to serious debate and challenge since its inception. Most recently, as cognitive approaches to perception have gained prominence, inference claims have become increasingly popular in philosophy, psychology, and computer science. It turns out, however, that there are a myriad conflicting senses of inference that are appealed to in these works. The goal of this essay is to explicate and clarify the concept of "perceptual inference" so as to resolve or dissolve the persistent controversies surrounding its use.

Chapter 4, I hope not too anachronistically, compares my account of Berkeley's views with those of the influential contemporary perceptual psychologist James J. Gibson. At several places in the first three chapters, I briefly recount various of Gibson's positions. Earlier drafts of chapters 1–3 had included more extensive treatments of the Gibsonian alternative. However, I now find that the presentation of the material goes more smoothly if I take out these remarks and treat them separately. Gibson saw Berkeley as one of the primary targets of his work. I think it provides a useful summary to examine significant, but overlooked, points of agreement between these two theorists, as well as to explore the more standardly cited points of contention. Such a review, I believe, can serve to untangle and clear up some of the quarrels over Gibson's much disputed claim that perception is direct.

Given the importance and current interest in the work of David Marr and his associates, there is comparatively little discussion of this material in my book. This is a reflection of the historical nature of parts of these essays and of the particular topics I consider, rather than an underestimation of the impact of these researches. Another reason is that I believe that many of the appeals to Marr's work to support a range of philosophical theses are misguided, a point highlighted by the fact that this theory is often cited by both proponents and opponents of the very same theses.[2] My doubts about the substance of certain of these more metaphysical issues is a theme that runs throughout this book, especially in chapters 3 and 4.

Although these four chapters contain a lot of historical material, my primary interest is in exploring how this background material can aid in understanding some persistent problems in the theory of vision. My discussion of Berkeley's *New Theory* is no substitute for the fuller commentary found in Armstrong's *Berkeley's Theory of Vision*[3] or for the detailed analysis and historical scholarship found in Margaret Atherton's *Berkeley's Revolution in Vision*.[4] Similarly, my remarks about the views of Hermann von Helmholtz are no substitute for an in depth consideration of his ideas and those of his contemporaries. Gary Hatfield's *The Natural and the Normative* provides an impressive study of some of this material.[5] Indeed, Atherton's and Hatfield's books fill in many of the historical gaps in my own essays and, I think, can serve to underwrite several claims and arguments that I simply allude to or assume.

Notes

1 All references to Berkeley's writings are to *The Works of George Berkeley, Bishop of Cloyne* (9 vols), ed. A. A. Luce and T. E. Jessop (Thomas Nelson, Edinburgh, 1948–57).
2 I raise some of these qualms in my short review of Marr's book *Vision* in *Philosophical Review*, 94 (1985), pp. 411–14.
3 D. M. Armstrong, *Berkeley's Theory of Vision* (Melbourne University Press, Melbourne, 1960).
4 Margaret Atherton, *Berkeley's Revolution in Vision* (Cornell University Press, Ithaca, NY, 1990). My account of Berkeley has benefited from the writings of numerous commentators. Of the more contemporary work, in addition to the books of Armstrong and Atherton, George Pitcher's *Berkeley* (Routledge and Kegan Paul, London, 1977), and C. M. Turbayne's Editor's Commentary in *George Berkeley, Works on Vision* (Bobbs-Merrill, Indianapolis, 1963), have been very useful.
5 Gary Hatfield, *The Natural and the Normative* (MIT Press, Cambridge, Mass., 1990).

1 Seeing Distance

The doctrine concerning the original and derivative functions of the sense of sight, which . . . is known as Berkeley's Theory of Vision, has remained, . . . one of the least disputed doctrines in the most disputed and most disputable of all sciences, the Science of Man . . . the warfare which has since distracted the world of metaphysics, has swept past this insulated position without disturbing it; and while so many of the other conclusions of the analytic school of mental philosophy . . . have been repudiated with violence by the antagonist school, that of Common Sense or innate principles, this one doctrine has been recognized and upheld by leading thinkers of both schools alike.[1]

So John Stuart Mill began his comments on Samuel Bailey. About 20 years later Thomas Abbott introduced his critical study of Berkeley's work on vision with a similar assessment of its status: "If we were challenged to point out a single discovery in mental science which is universally admitted, we should at once name the 'Theory of Vision' of Bishop Berkelely. Its success has been extraordinary. From the time of its first publication it has been accepted almost without question."[2]

Today many of Berkeley's claims have been disputed if not refuted, and quite understandably his views are not unanimously accepted by workers in the field. Still, one would be hard pressed to find many philosophical treatises that have had as profound and lasting an influence on the development of a science as has *An Essay Towards a New Theory of Vision*. Until recently, at least, it might have seemed reasonable to divide most psychological theories of the perception of the spatial properties of the world into two broad classes: those further elaborating a Berkeleian line and those reacting to and rejecting it. In turn, it is not at all unusual to find prominent reference to Berkeley's positions in current scientific books and theoretical papers on perception.

Although the *New Theory* contains an examination of a range of problems and topics, the aspect of Berkeley's theory most cited and most discussed has been his account of distance perception. And here Berkeley has come in for a beating of late. Perceptual psychologists have maintained that many of Berkeley's empirical claims and theoretical assumptions are no longer compatible with experimental data. At the same time, philosophers, when not questioning the very coherence of Berkeley's ideas, have sought to show that his arguments are unsound, in that they either rely on faulty epistemological and metaphysical premises or involve invalid reasoning.

Now, while many of these criticisms of Berkeley have a point, I believe that standard readings of Berkeley often misconceive the significance of crucial aspects of his psychology of perception and fail to appreciate the full force of his problems and proposals. Thus one can find psychological works which first argue that in light of the evidence one must reject Berkeley's thesis, but then go on to propose an account of the particular phenomenon that is quite in keeping with Berkeley's main ideas. In the philosophical literature, on the other hand, there is a tendency to read Berkeley's theory of vision with eyes pointed toward his subsequent idealism and immaterialism. The goal is to track down where Berkeley took the first fateful misstep that led to his startling (and "untenable") philosophical conclusions. Such emphasis on the supposed epistemological and metaphysical implications of Berkeley's position (especially when the philosophical issues themselves are discussed in terms of twentieth-century concerns that are not obviously Berkeley's) does not always provide the best context in which to understand his theory of vision. It often obscures where Berkeley's ideas fit into developments in the field of perception, while not adequately accounting for the fact, noted by Mill and Abbott, that Berkeley's theory of vision was accepted even by thinkers who found his subsequent philosophical views repugnant. Consequently, it leaves unexplained why Berkeley has played such a pivotal role in vision theory, and why he is frequently cited in contemporary psychological writings.

Perhaps the extent to which Berkeley's ideas have been differently understood and received can be highlighted by comparing a few quotations from representative philosophical and psychological works. Consider first the remarks of Alan Donagan and Julian Hochberg:

> Although Berkeley's theory of vision was generally received as true for over a century, so much of it depends on the false proposition that distance cannot be immediately seen that it has long been discredited.[3]

> The most influential theory of space perception in Western thought has been that distance is not a direct visual sensation at all.[4]

Donagan, along with numerous other philosophical commentators is convinced that the idea that distance perception is not immediate "has long been discredited." Yet, if one turns to a standard psychological text on vision, such as Hochberg's, one finds a much different assessment of the status of this claim. The following selections from George Pitcher and Hermann von Helmholtz are likewise in sharp contrast:

> Whatever a person immediately (or directly) sees he has incorrigible knowledge of. . . . Berkeley is firm in his espousal of [this] . . . Many philosophers through the ages have certainly accepted something like it as axiomatic.[5]

> We are not in the habit of observing our sensations accurately. . . . Thus in most cases some special assistance and training are needed in order to observe these latter subjective sensations.[6]

Pitcher is undoubtedly right when he says that many philosophers have taken it as axiomatic that we have incorrigible knowledge of our sensory states. But Helmholtz's account of our ability to report on our sense experience better reflects the position of most visual theorists working in the Berkeleian tradition, including, as I shall argue, Berkeley himself. The next quotations, from Bertrand Russell and James Sully, provide another striking case of conflicting viewpoints.

> Berkeley's theory of vision, according to which everything looks flat, is disproved by the stereoscope.[7]

> Some years ago it was commonly thought that, thanks to the arguments of the Berkeleyans aided by the experiments of Wheatstone and others the derivative nature of visual space was amply demonstrated.[8]

Russell has been joined by other critics in citing Wheatstone's invention of the stereoscope as a damaging blow to Berkeley's line of thought. The actual developments in visual theory, however, would not seem to support such a conclusion. As Sully points out, many, if not most, of the early stereoscope experiments were generally taken to confirm or strengthen Berkeley's position. Similar, disparate, if not contradictory, accounts of other ideas and key claims abound.

In this chapter I will attempt to place Berkeley's theory within a context of work in the scientific study of vision. Instead of asking "Where did Berkeley go wrong?," I will concentrate on the question "Where did Berkeley go right?" and examine those aspects of his theory of vision that formed the bedrock for a long tradition. When looked at from this perspective, I think it becomes clear that Berkeley's central claims are not particularly confused or empirically unmotivated or the sorts of claims likely to be abandoned in light of armchair philosophical analysis. Nor do they necessarily rely on outdated epistemological principles or defunct metaphysical presuppositions. They depend, rather, on views about optics, sensory physiology, mental processing, and learning that not only were part and parcel of the best science of Berkeley's day but have exerted considerable influence on modern work as well. Moreover, various of the problems that Berkeley considered have had a continuous role in theories of space perception. Many are alive today, and several of Berkeley's ideas concerning these problems may very well be as plausible as the alternative solutions now available. Finally, I believe that a broader understanding of Berkeley's concerns can lead us to think more carefully about some critical aspects of the problem of distance perception that have not received as much attention as they deserve.

By tracing these links to historical and ongoing work in the theory of vision, I hope to provide a basis for better evaluating what Berkeley's real contributions in this field were and were not. Such a background should also prove helpful when it comes to studying Berkeley's other, more "philosophical" doctrines and examining the ramifications which his ideas about vision may or may not have had for them. For I believe that we can best interpret and appreciate these later doctrines when they are located within the context of the scientific work that Berkeley reflected upon and actively participated in developing. These matters will only be touched on in this chapter, however.[9]

Distance is not Immediate

The passage in the *New Theory* that has been most scrutinized and has been the subject of severest criticism appears right at the beginning. In section 2 Berkeley says: "It is, I think, agreed by all that distance, of itself and immediately, cannot be seen. For distance being a line directed end-wise to the eye, it projects only one point in the fund of the eye, which point remains invariably the same, whether the distance be longer or shorter." In section 11 he goes on to say: "Now from sect. 2 it is plain that distance is in its own nature imperceptible, and yet it is perceived by sight." There has been much speculation in the literature about what Berkeley means here and why he would deny the obvious — that we see distance and see it immediately when we open our eyes. Elaborate possible lines of reasoning have been sketched purporting to explain how someone like Berkeley might have been led to adopt the seemingly implausible and false view that distance perception is not immediate.[10]

Before examining in detail the claims of sections 2, 11, and related passages, a few preliminary remarks will serve to orient the discussion. First, Berkeley nowhere denies that we can determine or evaluate distance by sight. His thesis is only that the process by which this is accomplished is of one sort, not another (i.e., not immediate). Second, Berkeley did not think that this point was original or controversial. As has been well reported, the passage in section 2 is essentially a paraphrase of a passage in William Molyneaux's *New Dioptrics*. What's more, Berkeley says straight out that the thesis that distance perception is not immediate is "agreed by all." The claim was not new, then, and Berkeley was correct in saying that it was standardly accepted by his contemporaries. So it would be most peculiar if Berkeleys fame and prominence in the field of vision were to rest specifically on his championing the idea that distance perception is not immediate, or if his *New Theory* were aimed primarily at establishing this claim.

It is important, nevertheless, to understand what this view comes to if we are to place Berkeley's work in its historical context and appreciate its significance for the theory of distance perception. And here, I think, it is helpful to separate several issues that can be easily run together. In particular, we should distinguish (1) Berkeley's account of what it is to have an idea or evaluation of distance, (2) the thesis that ideas of distance gained by sight are not immediate, and (3) the claim that, in and of itself, distance is imperceptible by sight. While discussions in the recent critical literature have tended to focus on (2), Berkeley himself was mainly concerned with (1) and (3) and the relationship between them. Claim 2 was generally accepted by workers in the field; it was Berkeley's versions of (1) and (3) that required explanation and defense.

Throughout his *New Theory* Berkeley presses the reader to think about what distance ideas are like, and hence what it means to be a distance-perceiver. Is it, for example, to have a certain type of visual experience, or is it to make abstract metric judgments, or what?[11] Put briefly, Berkeley's own position in the *New Theory* is that spatial perception in general and distance perception in particular are intimately related to movement, to the guidance and adjustment of behavior. Spatial ideas are, at root, not only sensory concepts, as opposed to abstract ideas or deliverances of reason; they are sensory concepts of a specific sort. The very content or meaning of any spatial idea lies, ultimately, in its *tangible* consequences. To know the distance to X is to have ideas about locomotion, ideas about how many paces it will take to get to X or how much effort it will take to reach out and touch X. It is not a matter of how things look phenomenally. Seeing distance requires only that environmentally appropriate motor ideas are derived from the flux of visual sensations, whatever these sensations are like qualitatively. An organism perceives distance to the extent that its visual experience serves to direct effectively its movements in the world.

Berkeley further argues that visual experience, in and of itself, has no spatial content. The spatial qualities we typically ascribe to visual experience are not inherent properties of these sensations in the way that color is a quality of these experiences. Therefore, we can have no purely visual idea of distance. Nor is it possible to acquire any other spatial ideas from visual experience alone. Whatever spatiality or spatial significance vision has is derivative, the result of learning to correlate visual experience with tangible ideas.

It is Berkeley's stress on the pragmatic significance of vision, as essentially a guide to movement and touch, that leads to his being cited as a precursor of behaviorist analyses of perception. More important historically, though, were Berkeley's claims that visual experience lacked inherent spatiality, that vision and touch did not share any common spatial qualities, and that all spatial ideas were based on or derived from the tangible senses. For these views provided the foundation for the development of anti-nativist, motor theories of vision, variations of which were to dominate the study of perception well into the twentieth century. Indeed, it is primarily for these ideas that Berkeley owes his place as a pivotal figure in the history of the science of vision. But more on such matters later; let us first return to thesis 2.

Immediate versus Non-Immediate Processes

For Berkeley, as for other vision theorists, the claim that some idea we
have is "not immediate" is an empirical claim about the kind of process
that leads to our having that idea. Ideas are not immediate when they are
the result of mental activity, of processes that have a mental or psychological component. By contrast, immediate ideas are ideas that are brought
to mind by purely non-mental goings-on. The processes that underlie
immediate ideas are, on this score, like those that underlie the output
of our kidneys and livers or are responsible for our blinking when air is
puffed in our eyes. Such processes may be simple, or they may be complex; but they are entirely organic or physiological in nature. They do not
involve anything that would be called a "mental operation." With non-
immediate ideas the situation is different. Not only is the end state, the
idea, mental, but one or more of the intermediate stages leading to our
having the idea itself has ideational or mental content.

Berkeley's own version of what makes a process mental (or in more
modern parlance "psychological" or "representational" or "cognitive") is,
of course, closely tied to the then and long prevalent identification of
mental states with conscious states. Mental processes were understood to
involve manipulating ideas, ideas which were themselves assumed to be
states of consciousness. In particular, then, the claim that we do not see
distance immediately amounts to the claim that the ideas of distance,
derived from sight, depend on mental operations. For Berkeley this comes
out to mean that these ideas of distance are brought to mind via some
other intermediate ideas. Light rays, along with certain movements and
adjustments of our eyes, cause us to have sensations (sensory ideas) S_1,
. . . , S_n, which in turn bring it about that we experience an idea, D, of
distance. The initial ideas of sense are immediate, the result of purely
physiological operations, whereas D is non-immediate, depending as it
does on $S_1, . . . , S_n$ to bring it about.

Berkeley offers an analogy to help clarify his model. Using a metaphor
that occurs also in Descartes and Locke, he likens the processing in spatial
perception to what takes place in language comprehension.[12] In order to
understand someone's speech, we must first hear what the person says. It
is the experience of hearing the word that triggers the appearance of the
idea that the word represents. The idea "cat" that comes to mind is not
immediate; it is the result of our having an intermediate idea, the auditory

experience of the utterance of the word "cat." In keeping with what had become common practice, Berkeley, too, allows that often we do not focus attention on these intermediate ideas and may not be readily aware that we are having them. We may "read through" the experience or sensation of the sign when our attention is directed to its significance. We may not take cognizance or remember the qualities of the experienced sound and, in the extreme, may not even be sure whether we heard the English "cat" or the French "chat." What typically concerns us is the content, the "cat" idea, not its sign. Furthermore, the process of one idea triggering another, in most cases of developed space perception, is automatic and exceedingly quick. It may be practically impossible for us to isolate or reflect on the qualities of the fleeting intermediate sensation.[13]

The contrast, then, between immediate and non-immediate ideas is based on the kind of process that brings the ideas to mind. The distinction Berkeley makes is peculiar neither to him nor to his time.[14] One or another version of the distinction has figured continuously and prominently in the development of theories of perception. Helmholtz's enormously influential *Treatise on Physiological Optics*, for example, is divided into three separate volumes. Volume 1 is on the refraction of light, the anatomy of the eye, the working of the eye's lens and musculature, etc. Volume 2, "The Theory of Sensations of Vision," is, as its title suggests, about sensations. By definition, sensations are understood to be what our sense organs contribute to experience prior to any elaboration by mind. The properties and qualities of sensations depend solely on the makeup of our sensory apparatus. No psychic activity or mental processing is involved in their production. They are immediate, matters of sense. The study of visual sensations, for Helmholtz, belongs to the domain of physiology. Sensations comprise that part of perception which has an explanation in, as he calls it, "organic" terms.

Helmholtz leaves for the third volume of the *Treatise on Physiological Optics* visual phenomena which he believes are dependent on psychic activity. These features of vision are not due to our physiological constitution per se, but involve mental processing. Intermediate mental states are implicated in their genesis. The material of Volume 3, Helmholtz says, falls within the proper study of psychology. He claims, though, that only a single type of psychological process is involved in all the phenomena he examines − namely, the association of ideas. And he spells out his model of perception with the help of a language analogy quite similar to Berkeley's.[15]

Reliance on some such contrast between kinds of visual processing appears in present-day discussions as well. In a recent paper, for instance, Shimon Ullman maintains that an immediate/non-immediate distinction lies "at the heart of the dispute between the theory of direct perception [the theory associated with James J. Gibson] and the computational/ representational approach [his own and David Marr's]." He characterizes the difference between these approaches in the following way. A direct (or immediate) perception account is suitable for cases where "further elaboration . . . would only be possible in physiological, but not in psychological terms." Ullman concludes: "If the extraction of visual information *can* be expounded in terms of psychologically meaningful processes and structures, then it cannot be considered immediate."[16]

While appeal to an immediate/non-immediate distinction has thus been a constant element in the science of vision, the exact nature of this dichotomy has changed as conceptions of the mental and what counts as evidence for psychological processing have evolved. For a long time it was quite common to hold, for example, that learning could have no effect on our sense organs, that the outputs of sense were physiologically fixed. The responses of sense might be altered by disease or fatigue but not by experience. So it was assumed that any perceptual phenomenon that showed the influence of learning could not be immediate, an aspect of sensation, but must be non-immediate, resulting from the elaboration of sensation by mental operations. Helmholtz explicitly adopted this principle; it seems implicit in Berkeley's work; and the view is still quite prevalent. Also Berkeley, Helmholtz, and perhaps most early twentieth-century theorists thought it appropriate to restrict the notion of the "mental" to processes involving items with some sort of conscious representation. More contemporary researchers are usually willing to cast the net of the psychological wider, allowing that mental processes often deal with "ideas" or cognitive representations that never penetrate consciousness. In tracing the historical path of Berkeley's doctrines, it is, therefore, important to keep in mind that theorists' understandings of various key concepts have not remained static. At the same time, it would be hard to appreciate what many of the controversies in visual science have been and are all about without taking cognizance of the supposed immediate/non-immediate distinction.[17]

Some Debates about Immediacy

We have already noted that Berkeley and his contemporaries assumed that distance perception was not immediate. But then which aspects of vision might fall into the category of immediate, and why? Color phenomena would be an obvious first candidate. It might seem only plausible that our having an experience of red when looking at a fire engine and blue when viewing the sky are fully determined by the interplay between the properties of the light striking our retina and the nature of our visual receptors. Associations built up by learning or complex cognitive operations have no role to play. Consider next the experience we have when we look at a piece of paper on which are inscribed two solidly colored figures, a small circle and a much larger square. These figures appear different in shape, and the square occupies more of our phenomenal field than the circle.[18] Here again, it might seem reasonable to suppose that these features of vision occur independently of any mental elaboration. The square stimulates more and different retinal areas than the circle, and our visual sense is simply set up to respond to these differences with qualitatively distinct sensations. It is not surprising, then, that Berkeley, along with many earlier and later theorists, took the distributions of color and light in our phenomenal field to be immediate, as opposed to non-immediate, properties of sight.

Still, I used the word "candidate" above for the label "immediate," and advisedly so. For the question of whether various visual facts are best explained organically (i.e., in terms of sensory physiology) or psychologically (i.e., in terms of intermediate mental processes) has been hotly contested throughout the modern history of perceptual studies. A few examples may give some of the flavor of these debates.

A piece of coal in sunlight or indoors looks black, while a lump of sugar in both situations looks white. Yet the sunlit coal reflects more white light than either it or the white-looking sugar reflect under indoor lighting conditions. Treating these phenomena as features of sensation is thus problematic, since it seems that there is no straightforward correspondence between the stimulus (the absolute light intensity) and the phenomenal quality (the experienced neutral color). Historically, two types of theories have been offered to explain these facts: those that claim that the phenomena are not immediate and those that have attempted to show

how they could be understood as sensations. Irvin Rock, describes these conflicting approaches as follows in his introductory text:

> The classical explanation of the constancy of neutral color (despite varying illumination) is that the level of illumination is taken into account in assessing the light an object reflects to the eye. Helmholtz suggested a process of this kind. Thus, for example, although a white object in dim illumination reflects little light, it is perceived to be receiving little illumination. Therefore, the low intensity of the retinal image may still be "thought" to emanate from an object of high reflectance.[19]

An alternative approach tries to explain the phenomena more peripherally, by adopting a radically different view of how sensory mechanisms function. The stimulus property determining the degree of experienced whiteness is taken to be not the absolute intensity of the light that the object reflects, but the relative intensities or ratios of the light coming from the object and those in its neighboring environment. On this account, "cognitive operations . . . are not necessary, but rather . . . sensory mechanisms suffice to explain constancy".[20] According to the classical view, the sensations of the coal differ under varying lighting conditions. But, due to mental processing, the sunlit sensation is read through, and the coal perceived as the same black in both circumstances. On the alternative approach, the constant black qualia are determined by the constant intensity *ratios* of the stimuli. No psychological work is needed; the experience is immediate, a matter of sense.

Another famous controversy concerned the explanation of color contrast phenomena. A patch of gray appropriately surrounded by red appears green. Mentalistic accounts, such as that preferred by Helmholtz, assumed that we have an immediate impression or sensation of gray which triggers the green perception. The reason for this happening is attributed to complex associative habits that develop as a result of frequently viewing objects through screens or other filters that alter the color of light. Those who deny that color contrast phenomena are psychic seek to explain these experiences directly, in terms of the workings of our sensory mechanisms. The stimuli from the red and the gray areas do not have the same effects when they occur in isolation as when they occur side by side. In the latter situation, the overall stimulus pattern results in low-level neural interactions of the sort that just produce a green sensation. No effects of learning or cognitive representation impinge on the process.

These conflicting approaches also turn up in discussions of spatial perception, the study of perceptual illusions and constancies being of particular interest, as they play an important role in the *New Theory*. Although the moon remains the same size and casts the same-size image on the retina, regardless of whether it is up above or on the horizon, it seems much bigger when on the horizon (this is called "the moon illusion"). By contrast, when a person walks away from us, although the size of the retinal image projected is reduced radically, the person does not appear to shrink (i.e., size constancy). One version of what goes on in both cases is that our sensations vary directly with the stimuli. For Berkeley, the number of minimum visibilia comprising the two moon scenes is the same, while the number of minimum visibilia comprising the person's image at different distances differs. The moon illusion occurs even though the phenomenal sizes are constant, because associative habits related to other aspects of the situation trigger unlike size ideas or evaluations. The reverse takes place with size constancy. Interpretive habits cause us to read through the changing sensations, giving us the veridical perception of unchanging size. Illusion and constancy are each non-immediate features of perception.[21] Critics of this psychic approach – for example, Gestaltists and Gibsonians – have argued that the visual appreciation of size is not to be understood along the lines of sign interpretation. Constancy and illusion do not depend in this way on the mental processing of visual sensations or other cognitive representations.

Examples of these contrasting approaches, early and recent, could be multiplied.[22] Suffice it to say that the tradition that came down from Berkeley stressed the importance of learning and psychic processing. Helmholtz, in fact, maintains in the *Treatise on Physiological Optics* that perhaps the major thing his research demonstrates is that many visual phenomena which other theorists had assumed to be sensations and amenable to organic explanation are better treated as psychological facts showing the influence of acquired associative habits. Which side, in the end, gained the upper hand in these various debates is a complicated matter, but one that need not be explored here. My concern, so far, has been only to provide background concerning the nature of the immediate/non-immediate distinction and the role it has played in visual science. But if, as I believe, Berkeley's use of this distinction is reasonably continuous with that characteristic of work in vision both before and after his *New Theory*, it might be appropriate to interpret his use in a manner consonant with this history. And from the material we have reviewed, it would seem that a proper understanding of such an immediate/non-immediate dichotomy would incorporate the following features:

1   Immediacy depends on the type of processing involved and not on the kind or nature of the idea. Color may be the paradigm case of an immediate object of sight. Yet, to the extent that the classic or psychic accounts of neutral color and color contrast are correct, some instances of color vision are not immediate. We cannot settle the question of the immediacy of an idea simply by appealing to epistemological principles, ordinary language practices, or everyday introspective reports.

2   While there are connections to be drawn, the immediate notion does not match up with our ordinary language "looks," "appears," and "seems" locutions. The sunlit coal *looks* black; the moon *appears* bigger on the horizon; the person *seems* to remain the same size several steps further away. None of these experiences would be immediate according to psychic theories. If, as is often said, sense-data are the sorts of things that have the properties that things appear to have, then these cases show that sense-data are not readily identified with immediate ideas.

3   There is also a related mismatch between the immediate/non-immediate dichotomy and certain epistemological distinctions between types of claims or statements. It has been proposed, for example, that when we say that things merely look to be in a certain way, without committing ourselves to how things really are in the world, we are talking about what we see immediately.[23] But this need not be so. We may protect against factual error by claiming that the cat *seems to be* 3 feet away rather than asserting that it *is* 3 feet away, just as we can avoid commitment as to the real color of the fire engine by saying only that it looks red. The red look, for someone like Berkeley, is immediate, but the 3-foot awayness of the appearance is not. And on the classic account of neutral color, we are not reporting what we immediately see when we speak guardedly and say only that the sunlit coal seems to me to be black.

4   Immediate ideas of sense did not typically have the epistemological status frequently assigned to them in twentieth-century philosophical discussions of the foundations of knowledge or in discussions of the mind–body problem. For Berkeley, as well as for later vision theorists, although our immediate experiences are mental states, states of consciousness, we are not necessarily aware of their qualities in the sense that we can accurately report on them. We may not realize what our real immediate color experience is when we look at the sunlit coal or the gray patch

with its red surround. Similarly, appreciation of the extent of our phenomenal field actually occupied may be erroneous, once we become gripped
by the moon illusion or have achieved perceptual size constancy. Long-
ingrained habits of "reading through" may prevent us from being able to
reflect or report correctly on these sensory mental states. Helmholtz is not
alone (see Helmholtz quote earlier in the chapter) in cautioning that such
processes of interpretation make getting data about the real nature and
qualities of our sensations one of the most difficult tasks in vision research. Only those highly skilled in introspection will be able to provide
this information with any degree of accuracy. Everyday, ordinary reports
of sensory states are not, in general, certain; they can be mistaken, and
they are often corrigible. Science may override individual reports with the
help of the introspections of others better trained at the task or on the
basis of empirical principles about learning and sensory physiology. In
the scientific study of perception, incorrigibility has not been assumed to
be an obvious property of sensory states.[24]

The Optic Writers

Given this understanding of the immediate/non-immediate dichotomy,
we can then see what Berkeley is doing when, having just said in section
2 of the *New Theory* that all agree that distance is not immediate, he
launches an attack on the so-called optic writers.[25] The basic issues at stake
can be understood with the help of a few examples similar to the ones
Berkeley discusses. Suppose our eyes, one located at point A and the other
at point B, are turned (converge) to fixate on a point C. The size of the
angles formed, CAB and CBA, are a function of the distance to C, becoming larger the further C is from us. If we know the values for CAB, CBA,
and the distance between our eyes, AB, it is possible to compute geometrically the distance to C. Consider next another relationship between
optical facts and distance, this time involving only a single eye. When a
point C is far away, the light rays from C that strike the perceiver's lens
will be approximately parallel to each other. As C approaches, the packet
of light will contain nonparallel rays, the amount of divergence being
inversely proportional to the distance. In order for the light from C to be
focused at a single point on the retina, the lens or other ocular mechanisms must adjust (accommodate) accordingly; otherwise the image of C
will be blurred. It is possible to compute the distance to C on the basis

of information about the angles and amount of divergence of the light rays.

In the *New Theory*, Berkeley is more than willing to acknowledge such geometrical/optical facts. Berkeley's complaint against the optic writers is not over the optics and relevant geometry but over the psychological model he thought they endorsed. Berkeley understood them to be claiming that we perceive short distances by processes akin to the way that a surveyor measures distances. Taken literally, this means that we actually have explicit ideas about the size of the various angles and use this initial size information to compute distance via the appropriate geometrical formulas. The ideas that the model appealed to as data must be distinguished, then, from visual blur or the sensory ideas of muscle strain and movement that accompany convergence and accommodation. The data were taken instead to be abstract ideas of spatial measure. Likewise, the computational formulas employed in the model were not to be understood as descriptions of sensory or empirical regularities, but were to be taken as theorems of mathematical geometry, reflecting necessary connections among ideas. They were knowable a priori, the product of reason or "a kind of innate geometry."[26] In turn, the idea of distance derived from these calculations would itself be an abstract idea, not one of sensory origin and content.

Berkeley finds this model of distance perception unacceptable. It postulates a specific type of mental processing that he believes does not take place. He thinks that his opponents have been led to make this mistake by failing to distinguish appropriately the claims of geometrical optics from a psychological account of what goes on in perception. In more modern parlance, one might say that Berkeley thought that the optic writers' principles and computations were not "psychologically real." Berkeley's own theory involves mental processing too, but of a different type. It appeals only to sensory experience and processes of association, one idea suggesting another. We learn to correlate the sensations of convergence, accommodation, and certain qualities of our visual experience with varying distance ideas. There are, however, no necessary connections between these sensations and the distance ideas they trigger; nor, Berkeley later argues, is there any likeness between them. Sensations of muscle strain, blur, and haziness of color are not at all like ideas of distance. So we cannot by means of a priori reasoning, or by means of similarity, come to appreciate the latter by experiencing the former. Were our eyes to be arranged differently or our lens to refract light differently, the correlations we would have to master would be different, and that is all there is to the matter.

While Berkeley's underlying motive for rejecting the optic writers' model may well have been metaphysical, an objection to abstract ideas, his arguments against it are very much empirical. First, Berkeley does not think that a reasonable story can be told of how we are able to obtain the sort of explicit geometrical data needed to perform the relevant computations. As just noted, in order for the geometrical principles to be used, angle size information must first be registered. But all the perceiver has to go on initially in the binocular case are the muscle tensions and contractions arising from convergence. These produce sensations of strain and movement, not explicit ideas of angle size. Similarly, our sense of sight does not register directly the variations in the angles of the light rays that emanate from an object. What we actually sense are the muscle adjustments that accompany accommodation. Berkeley also argues that the angles and lines which the optic writers talk about are, strictly speaking, formal abstractions, not real existents in and of themselves, the kind of objects capable of stimulating the sense organs.

Second, Berkeley claims that introspection does not reveal us having ideas of angle size and computations over these ideas. It may be thought that Berkeley is being inconsistent here in using introspective data to refute the optic writers, since in perceiving we tend to be unaware of having the muscle sensations to which his own model appeals.[27] Now although Berkeley could undoubtedly have been more careful in these passages, I do not believe his use of introspective evidence is patently self-defeating. Earlier it was pointed out that practically all theorists allowed that we may not be aware of sensory states when we are reading through them. And this is surely how Berkeley and most everyone else understood the fate of the sensations of convergence and accommodation. What's more, if we focus attention on convergence and accommodation changes, we do become aware of the muscle sensations employed by Berkeley's model. In addition, blur, perspective, interposition, and so on, the standardly cited "pictorial" signs of distance, were assumed to be aspects of our visual experience. The same cannot be said for the optic writers' intermediate ideas. We cannot find these geometrical ideas in experience, and as discussed above, we have no physiological story to account for how they could be registered, let alone one that independently recommends their postulation. Berkeley also relies on another difference between the two models to bolster his position. Whereas it may seem reasonable to suppose that simple, rapid, associative processes can take place and escape our awareness, it is less plausible to assume that the complex computations, the optical theory postulates, could go on in our mind unnoticed.

Berkeley, however, does not rest his argument against the optic writers either on introspection or on assumptions about what kinds of ideas could possibly be in the minds of perceivers. He devotes relatively few words to this line of criticism. He spends much more time trying to show that the optic writers' approach cannot account for certain empirical perceptual phenomena readily handled by his own theory. Thus, he devotes a full 12 sections of the *New Theory* to a discussion of Barrow's case, a visual phenomenon that many of the optic writers themselves took to be incompatible with their theories.[28] Berkeley believes, however, that Barrow's phenomenon can be explained satisfactorily on his own model. Berkeley's long discussion of the moon illusion is aimed at a similar point. The optic writers, he argues, have no acceptable basis for explaining the illusion, while he does. Therefore, Berkeley claims, empirical evidence and good scientific practice favor his account.

Whether one finds Berkeley's characterization of the optic writers' position completely accurate or his criticisms convincing, Berkeley is raising here, early on in the history of psychology, a problem of general interest concerning the nature of psychological explanation. Berkeley is questioning the relationship between formal models of a competence and accounts of the actual psychological processing. The problem he focuses on is much of a piece with current controversies about the psychological reality of grammars, as well as more recent debates over the status and psychological relevance of certain computer vision programs. In any case, a study of scientific work in Berkeley's own time and before indicates that there was often much confusion and a running together of physical theory with psychological accounts. Perceptual psychology was not readily separated from studies of optics, and claims and assumptions about optics were uncritically incorporated into hypotheses about vision.[29] Failure to distinguish features of the two types of theories led to major problems, perhaps the most significant of which was the puzzle over the inverted retinal image. Numerous attempts to formulate a satisfactory optical theory had been frustrated because the correct solution entails that the retinal image be inverted. This result was assumed to be untenable, since we perceive objects as upright. After Kepler demonstrated that the retinal image was in fact inverted, many workers thought it necessary to assume that the visual system had a means to right the otherwise upside-down

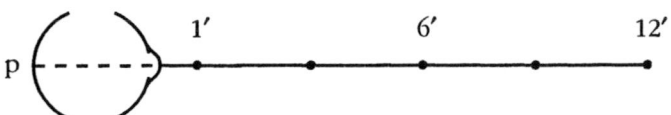

Figure 1.1   *The one-point argument. Any point along a line of sight projects an image to the same retinal point p.*

display. In the *New Theory* Berkeley shows how this puzzle, as well as others the optic writers faced, can be dissolved once we adequately distinguish optical theory from psychological explanation. One of the contributions of the *New Theory* to the study of vision was to notice and stress the importance of being clear about this distinction.

Disputes between Berkeley and the optic writers over the correct model of distance perception should not obscure, however, the fact that Berkeley is on firm ground when he says that "all agree" that seeing distance is not immediate. Berkeley and the optic writers differ mainly over which model of *non-immediate* processing is the right one. And even here Berkeley's dispute with the optic writers is fairly circumscribed. He points out in section 3 of the *New Theory* that since convergence and accommodation and the geometrical relationships on which they depend are of no help with more remote objects, the eyes do not converge and the light rays are for all practical purposes parallel, the optic writers too must rely on such features as familiarity, size, and faintness, to determine the distances of objects. But these features are admittedly contingent signs of distance, and the correlations do not represent necessary connections among ideas.

The One-Point Argument

Why is it, though, that everyone agrees that distance is not immediate? The argument Berkeley offers is a one-liner that comes directly from the optic writers themselves. It was all the argument that seemed needed to gainsay the point. Following Kepler's optical discoveries, it had become clear that "distance being a line directed end-wise to the eye it projects only one point in the fund of the eye, which point remains invariably the same whether the distance is larger or shorter." (See figure 1.1.) A point at any distance along a line of sight projects the same single point p on the retina. The light striking p could be from an object at 1 foot, 6 feet,

12 feet, and so on. It is also the case that the spatial extent between the object and our eye is not displayed anywhere in the retinal image. When the three-dimensional world is mapped onto our two-dimensional retina, nothing in the retinal image "directly" presents or represents this distance itself. There is, in turn, no extent exhibited in the visual sensation corresponding to differences in distance *along a line of sight*.

Now some commentators have tried to explain the rationale and role of the one-point argument in terms of the indeterminateness of the stimulus, the fact that the stimulus at point p is ambiguous as to the distance of its source.[30] And surely such geometrical ambiguity is an important fact that must be dealt with by any theory of vision. Nevertheless, emphasizing this aspect of the one-point argument can be misleading, and Berkeley, for one, does not talk about the problem specifically in these terms. The reason is that the claim that distance is non-immediate does not depend critically on the assumption of stimulus ambiguity. The one-point argument is not meant to preclude the possibility that some feature of the visual stimulus correlates unambiguously and determinately with distance. To see this, suppose, for example, that our experience of brightness depends on a property of light that varies directly with distance. A given degree of brightness would then correspond unambiguously with the distance to its source. Still, these different sensations of brightness would not, in and of themselves, be ideas of distance. They would remain immediate ideas of brightness that could serve only as *signs* of distance. Line-of-sight distance itself would not be displayed in the retinal image or its accompanying sensation.[31]

What the one-point argument shows is that distance perception is not direct, in that it depends first on registering non-distance ideas, then on using them to derive ideas about how far away things are. The situation is different when it comes to our ideas of color. A change in an object's color will alter the properties of the stimulus in ways that directly affect the color of the sensation. Color can show up as a feature of the visual experience itself, and in the case of simple color perception at least, may be explained in terms of physiological mechanisms, without having to appeal to intermediate, psychic steps. It was largely acceptance of this analysis of the problem of distance perception that led to everyone's agreeing that seeing distance is not an immediate process. The problem clarified itself more fully as a problem with developments in the theory of optics, culminating in and subsequent to the discoveries of Kepler about the formation of the retinal image and the role of the retina in vision. The issues do not arise in the same way in earlier analyses that claimed that three-dimensional copies ("eidolas") of the world enter our sensorium, or on accounts that postulated light rays of varying lengths emanating from the eye to the object.[32] Once the correct account of the optics and function of the retina had been worked out, however, the one-point argument proved compelling.

Berkeley's response to the problem for distance vision posed by the one-point argument has, in part, been touched on and needs only to be briefly reviewed. We perceive distance on the basis of cues or clues that we have learned to correlate with distance. The cues, like words, are signs that we interpret for their significance. Several distinct types of cues play a role in distance perception. The sensations resulting from convergence and accommodation are, strictly speaking, nonvisual. These eye adjustments produce stimuli that are registered by receptors geared to detect muscle tension or movement, not light. Their effects are initially recorded by our tangible sense. The other cues to distance are due to our light (or visual) sense, and they show up as features of our experienced visual sensations. Among these are the blurring of images of objects too close to be properly focused, image size, and the "pictorial cues" of interposition, perspective, height in field, and the like. Familiarity also plays a considerable role, but its effects involve even more complicated processing. While Berkeley reserves a special place for convergence, accommodation, and blur, a fact to which we shall return, he nowhere denies the importance of these other sources of information. They are, after all, the only thing we have to go on in perceiving more remote objects.

In sum, the one-point argument convinced Berkeley, along with almost everyone else, that seeing distance could not be immediate. Berkeley adopted a two-stage sign or cue model of the process. Visual ideas of distance come to us by way of intermediate mental steps, the prior sensing or registering of non-distance features of the situation that indicate distance. Here, then, lies the main empirical content of the claim in the *New Theory*, section 2, that distance is not immediately seen.

But if this is so, Berkeley was promoting a position with a good deal of staying power. For the force of the one-point argument has proved hard to resist, and the typical response to it has been much the same as Berkeley's. Through most of the history of theories of vision it has been generally accepted that distance perception is not a direct or immediate process and that some version of a cue model is the correct approach. Even recent texts set out the issue in terms not very different from those found in the *New Theory*. Here, for example, is how Irvin Rock structures the discussion at the beginning of a chapter on distance vision.

> The problem of the perception of the third dimension arises from the observation that the retina can be considered a two-dimensional surface, so that distance per se is not recorded in the retinal image.... How then do we obtain information about distance? ... It is customary ... to list all the so-called clues or cues that might provide such information.[33]

Rock then goes on to examine the wide assortment of cues that have been proposed to play a role in distance perception. As is standard in such textbooks, he distinguishes pictorial from motor cues, and discusses the relative effectiveness of the cues and what happens when the cues conflict. He also calls attention to the fact that if an object is presented in a way that eliminates all the cues, we are no longer able to determine its distance. While we see its color, it does not look to be at any specific distance. It is worth mentioning too that when Rock in later chapters takes up simple color perception, terms like "cue," "clue," and "sign" are nowhere to be found.

Now in my view there are some interesting issues concerning the soundness of the cue-model approach and reasons to worry that it may be circular or non-explanatory at crucial points. Furthermore, within cue models there are differences on such matters as how people conceive of the registration of the cues (if cues must be experienced as sensations or if the information may be represented in some other way), whether the underlying processes are like the optic writers' computations or simply associative linkages, and so on. And each of these versions may be ranked as more or less compatible with Berkeley's own theory. I think it fair to say, however, that well into the twentieth century, a large percentage of theorists treated the cues as sensations and the processing as more or less associative. Historically, the major debates were not here, but over the extent to which spatial perception is learned or innate. If Berkeley fell for the one-point argument and took it to imply that seeing distance was not an immediate but a psychic process, so did almost everyone else. An indication of the compelling nature of the one-point argument is that it was not until the 1950s, primarily with the work of James J. Gibson, that an alternative proposal for distance perception gathered much support. As Gibson was later to remark, the one-point argument "states the problem of perception of the third dimension, or depth perception, as it has been studied and puzzled over for 250 years."[34]

Distance is not an Idea of Sight

While Berkeley may be most remembered for saying that distance is not immediate, this claim is really just the starting point of his theory of vision. Berkeley's more original and more controversial ideas are to be found elsewhere, in the implications he drew from the non-immediate doctrine and especially in his claims about the nature and acquisition of our spatial ideas. For Berkeley not only maintained that the process by which we see distance is mental; he also went on to argue that our visual experience lacks any inherent qualities of spatiality from which we could derive our ideas of space. This latter claim, although related, is different from the claim that spatial perception is non-immediate.

To see this, consider again the psychic theory of color contrast. On this account, color contrast is a two-step process; the gray sensation leads us to have a green idea. The green idea, however, is an idea originally acquired by our sense of sight. It is a trace of this earlier visual experience that is now revived. Color contrast is not immediate, but the secondary color idea is the sort of idea perceptible by sight. Berkeley maintains that the situation is entirely different in the case of distance. In distance perception, the second-stage idea we derive from the immediate sensation is not a visual idea at all; nor is it a construct or combination of visual ideas, or in any way derivable from visual experience by reason, similarity, or analogy. According to Berkeley, when we look about and determine the distance of some object, the distance idea we attribute to the object is, strictly speaking, a tangible idea.[35] Our everyday concept of distance in general is derived from movement experience, not sight, and the content or significance of any specific distance idea is entirely tangible. Visual experience itself has *no* intrinsic spatiality. Whatever spatiality we typically associate with visual phenomena is wholly derivative, a function of their signifying ideas of motion and touch. An organism that only had visual experience would not so much as have our ordinary concept of distance, let alone be able to judge correctly how far off things are.

The negative side of Berkeley's point may be made more strikingly by analogy with our sense of smell.[36] Experiences of odor may differ along a variety of dimensions, but color would not seem to be one of them. We cannot acquire ideas of color from our sense of smell. We may, of course, be able to determine by smell that an object is yellow, if we have come to link lemony smells with the yellow experience we have when looking at lemons. Nonetheless, yellow is not a property of the olfactory sensation itself. The odor and correlated visual experience do not share some common yellow quality, and it would not be possible to derive the idea of yellow by reasoning about the lemony odor. Likewise, it would seem that distance is not a quality of the sensations that our odor sense provides. We would not be able to develop our concept of distance if we were limited to information from this sense alone. We may acquire the ability to determine distance by correlating decreases and increases in the intensities of smells with our experience of moving toward and away from lemons. But the odors themselves have no distance dimension; they do not share distance qualities with the associated sensations arising from movement.

That our sensations of smell have odor qualities but no color, while our visual experiences have color qualities but lack odor, are not points Berkeley would have seen the need to argue. What Berkeley wants to convince the reader of would appear more problematic. He wishes to maintain that vision is like smell with respect to distance. Distance is no more an aspect of visual experience than it or color are dimensions of our olfactory field. We could not derive our concept of spatial distance from visual experience alone or with only the added help of reason. Again, we may acquire the ability to evaluate distance by associating visual sensations and nonvisual ocular sensations with movement, but the visual sensations themselves have no inherent distance properties. They do not share distance qualities with our motor sensations.

Berkeley's main reason for insisting that vision plays a strictly derivative role in the acquisition of our idea of spatial distance and in its evaluation stems largely from considerations regarding the one-point argument. Berkeley assumed, as was standard, that the sensations from one sense modality could not effect the qualities of the sensations resulting from the stimulation of another modality. While the sensations due to accommodation and convergence may be used in determining distance, they cannot directly alter the way in which our visual sense responds to light. A particular array of light will produce, immediately, the same visual sensation no matter what sensations are produced by the mechanisms we have for sensing muscle contractions. But we also know that a point projected on our retina will remain "invariably the same whether the distance is longer or shorter." As explained above, the distance along a line of sight from the retinal point p to its stimulus source is not presented in the retinal image. Since the same holds for all the other points comprising the image, there is no representation in the retinal image of the third dimension *as such*. Nothing, for example, in the retinal and visual images reflects absolute distance by growing bigger or smaller in the way that the actual distance may increase or decrease. Vision is like smell. There are no inherent distance qualities to our visual sensations that match or are similar to our ideas of spatial distance, as there are color qualities that correspond to our color ideas. While there are intrinsically red and blue visual sensations, there could be no such thing as an intrinsically 1-foot versus 3-foot versus 12-foot visual sensation.

We may, of course, read through these visual sensations and thereby have different ideas of distance, but these "secondary" ideas, unlike those of color contrast, are not themselves initially visual ideas, ideas of our light sense. The optic writers, after all, had admitted as much. On their account, too, our ideas of spatial distance are not really visual; they depend on geometrical reasoning. Berkeley argued that the optic writers' model was unsatisfactory. Failure to distinguish carefully optics from psychology had led them in to error in thinking that they had an adequate account of the nature of our idea of distance. But if vision alone or vision plus reason was not the source of spatial ideas, where could these ideas come from? Berkeley's answer was that our ideas of space are due to our tangible sense. The very content of our idea of distance is its tangible significance. Thus the distance ideas we determine by sight are not only sensory, but derivative, parasitic on experience of movement and touch.

The Dimensions of Visual Space

Intuitively, this does not seem right. Vision seems very different from smell; there appears to be something inherently spatial to our visual sensations. So how can Berkeley and his followers deny the obvious facts of experience and maintain that our visual sensations are really flat, rather than voluminous or three-dimensional? Well, the first thing to note is that Berkeley never made this latter claim. Others did, and others often attributed this position to Berkeley. But in sections 158 and 159 of the *New Theory* Berkeley explicitly rejects the view that our visual sensations are flat; nor does he maintain that they were flat at birth. In fact, Berkeley denies that the claim that the immediate objects of vision are planes rather than solids makes literal sense.

D. M. Armstrong attempts to explain these passages along the following lines:

> [F]latness presupposes the existence of three dimensions, for it is only *surfaces* which can be said to be flat or not flat, and surfaces must be surfaces of *volumes*, and volumes are three-dimensional. Now Berkeley denies that objects are immediately seen as three-dimensional, and so he must deny they are seen as flat. But this is by no means incompatible with saying that the immediate objects of sight are ordered in two dimensions, for a merely two-dimensional manifold is not *flat*.[37]

On the basis of this analysis, Armstrong believes that he can square these later sections of the *New Theory* with his claim that Berkeley really held that "what is immediately seen forms a two-dimensional spatial field, . . . what is sometimes referred to as a 'flat image'." But if visual space is two-dimensional not three-dimensional it means, Armstrong says, that "I can see immediately that the man is to the left of the tree, and that the leaves of the tree are above its trunk (more strictly, all I immediately see are certain man-like, leaf-like, and trunk-like coloured shapes arranged in this way), but I cannot immediately see that the tree-like shape is more, or less, distant than the man-like shape."[38]

Although Armstrong's treatment of the flatness issue seems to me more correct than most, it has some problems. In particular, I do not think it captures fully the force or flavor of Berkeley's thesis. To see what Berkeley is getting at in sections 158 and 159, it is important to keep in mind that these passages occur near the end of the *New Theory*. Indeed, at this stage, Berkeley believes that he has established that the content of *all* our everyday spatial ideas is, in the end, tangible. Just as physical distance is measured in terms of tangible units, and what we mean by an object's size and shape are its tangible extent and outline, similarly direction is the idea of where we must turn to approach it, while planeness or solidity is a question of whether or not the object is uniformly smooth to the touch. Vision alone, or vision plus reason, will not provide the kinds of ideas needed and used in our understanding of physical space. So, for example, our idea of a physical circle is not to be identified with or derived from our visual experience of a circle viewed straight on. This visual idea is no more what we mean by "spatial circularity" than are any of the "elliptical" fields we visually experience when viewing a physical circle from most other orientations.

Berkeley, however, does not subscribe to the position which some

theorists were later to adopt, that our visual field has no intrinsic organization, that what we see originally are independent color elements having
no relationship to one another. But, for Berkeley, to allow that our visual
field has inherent structure does not mean that it makes sense to treat it
as a *spatial* realm to which our ordinary geometric ideas of physical space
can be non-metaphorically and meaningfully applied or from which they
can be derived. To think otherwise is to confuse physical space with
visual "space" in ways that lead to a set of problems which Berkeley had
sought to resolve earlier in the *New Theory*.

The dilemma of the inverted image, which Berkeley discussed in sections 88–119, is an important case in point. We say, for example, that
the man in front of us looks erect, but then are puzzled by the fact that
the image of him on our retina is inverted. The puzzle dissolves when we
realize that it makes no sense to describe our phenomenal visual field as
itself erect or upside down, as if it were located in the same space as the
retinal image and could be compared to it with respect to some common
idea of spatial orientation. We can, of course, come to use visual information in determining whether an object is pointing up or down; but
this is derivative, dependent upon correlations with the tangible. We
could not develop our ordinary ideas of spatial orientation from visual
experiences alone. Such experiences lack any intrinsic qualities of spatial
upness or downness to serve as a basis for acquiring these concepts.

Our ideas of direction receive a similar analysis. We may be tempted
to think that when we report that we see a red light off to the left, we
are locating the experienced quality in the spatially left half of our phenomenal field and that this visual left corresponds in direction to tangible
or spatial leftness. This too is a confusion. Our visual field has no such
inherent property as spatial leftness or rightness. Visual experience can
serve to indicate spatial direction only because we have established contingent correlations between eye, head, and body motions and changes
in what occupies our visual field. Visual sense alone cannot provide the
experience necessary to develop our ideas of spatial direction. *Contra*
Armstrong, we do not see spatial orientation and direction immediately,
any more than we immediately see distance. Visual experience has no
intrinsic geometrical features corresponding to, or in common with, our
spatial ideas of location.

In the passages preceding section 158, Berkeley argues that the
situation is similar with respect to our concepts "plane" and "solid." He
attempts to drive home this conclusion with a thought experiment

involving a spirit that has only a visual sense. Although the spirit could have a full range of visual sensations just like our own, it would have no means of registering touch or movement. Berkeley believes that it follows from earlier considerations about distance perception that such a spirit could not have our idea of spatial distance, of how far off in space something is, for this, he thinks he has shown, is essentially a tangible idea. But without an idea of distance, the spirit could not have our ordinary concepts of spatial plane or solid, which are defined in terms of distance relations. Berkeley believes, however, that it is a mistake to conceive of the spirit's visual sensations as being, therefore, qualitatively flat, in the way, say, the surface of a painting is flat. Rather, he maintains, the spirit would experience an array of color and light that does not itself have spatial dimensions or character of the sort used to describe physical space. The organization of the spirit's visual experience would be *sui generis*. His sensations would no more be properly described as spatially flat than as voluminous. These spatial concepts simply do not apply to the spirit's visual sensations, or to ours for that matter. Like "up" and "down," or "left" and "right," "plane" and "solid" are not inherent qualities of visual experience in the way color is. Visual experience is literally neither flat nor voluminous. Neither we nor the spirit could acquire our ordinary spatial concepts of "plane" and "solid" on the basis of such experience alone.

At the same time, Berkeley is not committed to the view that flat objects generally look the same as three-dimensional ones. We can, without incoherence, give meaning to the notion that plane objects look planar and solids solid, just as we can provide a non-problematic reading of the claim that the red light looks or appears to be to our left. All we mean in the latter case is that we have come to assign leftward tangible significance to the visual experience. We run into trouble only if we assume that this spatial leftness is nonderivative, a property of the visual field itself, or if we assume that what we derivatively call "visually left" shares some directional sensory quality with our experience of tangible left.

The same applies to our experience of planes and solids. Those sensations that serve as signs of spatial planes we take to calling "planar," while those we interpret as signaling solids we label "solid."

> What we strictly see are not solids, nor yet planes variously coloured: they
> are only diversity of colours. And some of these suggest to the mind solids,

and others plane figures, just as they have been experienced to be connected with the one or the other: So that we see planes in the same way
we see solids, both being equally suggested by the immediate objects of
sight, which accordingly are themselves denominated planes and solids.
But though they are called by the same names with things marked by
them, they are nevertheless of a nature intirely different.[39]

Something looks flat if it has a look we associate with its being that
of a spatially flat surface, and something looks solid if its appearance has
solid significance for us. The sensations we have of a circle differ typically
from those we have of a sphere. We can appreciate this by considering
how we would draw pictures of the two figures. The circle might be best
illustrated with a simple circular line. To illustrate a sphere, shading
might be added to model the depth. Our visual experience of this shading
is usually enough to lead us to associate or read depth significance into
such a figure. In turn, the look or appearance of the circle illustration
is labeled "flat," and that of the shaded figure "solid." If the sphere illustration contains additional cues to the third dimension, the experience
we have of it will even more readily lead us to assign depth significance
and hence to describe it as having depth. No problem arises in distinguishing the look of planes from that of solids, as long as we recognize
the derivative nature of these labels. The visual sensations themselves are
literally neither spatially flat nor solid.

As indicated, Berkeley claims that vision not only lacks intrinsic properties of distance, flatness, and solidity, but that all its seemingly spatial
properties are really derivative. While the first 51 sections of the *New Theory*
are primarily concerned with distance, the next 100 or so sections are
devoted to showing that matters are similar with respect to the acquisition and evaluation of magnitude, shape, motion, orientation, and direction. Our ideas of these spatial properties are not derivable from sight;
nor are they attainable by reason with the aid of sight as the optic writers
might argue. Vision can provide information about magnitude, situation,
shape, and motion only as the result of contingent correlations with
tangible sensations of movement.

Berkeley's arguments in each of these later cases require more than
an appeal to the one-point doctrine, and the details and complexities of
these arguments cannot be gone into here.[40] Suffice it to say that some of
Berkeley's most impressive work on vision is to be found in these sections. The positions he espoused on the inverted image, the Molyneux

problem, and the lability of our visual system, among a host of other issues, served to stimulate a line of empirical research and theoretical debate that has continued to this day. Berkeley's account of these other spatial ideas forms an essential part of what, I have argued earlier, were his more original and important contributions to the study of vision – namely, his anti-nativist, motor theory of spatial perception. According to Berkeley, our spatial visual abilities require not only learning, but learning of a very special kind. They depend on ideas that can be gained only by movement and touch.

Alternative Theories

Although Berkeley's critique of the optic writers was widely accepted, his account of the derivative nature of visual space perception did not go unchallenged. Especially on the Continent, there was a strong attraction to what came to be called the "Kantian" view, the view that spatiality is imposed by the mind on sensory experience. Our basic idea of space is not derived from sense, nor, as the optic writers would have it, by the use of reason; rather, it is a form of intuition that constitutes a precondition for meaningful perception. As William James characterized it, the Kantian position was that "there is a *quality produced* out of the inward resources of the mind, to envelop sensations which, as given originally, are not spatial."[41]

Another seriously explored alternative to the Berkeleian position, varieties of which were championed by Ewald Hering, Carl Stumpf, and William James, agreed with Berkeley that our idea of space is not a "Kantian" a priori imposition of mind on sense, but rejected the Berkeleian claim that spatial ideas could only be derived from touch and movement. Most radically, James argued that all our sensations, including odor, taste, and sound, have a voluminous quality of their own, which can serve as a basis for constructing our conception of space. But for James, too, spatial *distance* is not an immediate quality of visual sensations. His claim is only that we can use the sensed voluminousness of vision in conjunction with our experience of objects as we or they move about to build a sensory, albeit visual, idea of space. "The measurement of distance is, as Berkeley truly said, a result of suggestion and experience. But visual experience alone is adequate to produce it."[42]

The major empirical upshot of both these challenges to the Berkeleian position was the claim that certain aspects of spatial vision do not require learning, and hence are innate. More empirical work and theoretical energy was devoted to exploring these innateness issues than to any other issues in the field. The "nativists" and "empiricists" split over a range of phenomena, including such matters as whether bare extensivity or spread-outness of visual experience is learned; whether when we look at the following set of dots, : . : , we originally experience five unrelated phenomenal points and only with practice correlating retinal locations with eye movements experience the points aligned as we do; whether each point carries with it a sensational quality of location as well as color, and so forth.[43] It is important to keep in mind, however, that even among the nativists few theorists assumed that distance perception was innate or that anything that could be called "distance experiences" were qualities of simple visual sensations. The controversies were primarily about raw extensivity, relative location, and direction. And while the nativists' theories had their impact, the Berkeleian approach tended to dominate. "The most influential theory of space perception in Western thought has been that distance is not a direct visual sensation at all. Instead . . . memories of the grasping or walking motions that have been made in the past . . . provide the idea of 'distance.'"[44]

Binocular Disparity

Granted Berkeley never claimed that visual experience is flat or spatially two-dimensional; nonetheless, it has been maintained that Berkeley's arguments for a derivative theory of vision are fatally flawed by his failure to take adequately into account that normal perception involves the use of two eyes. Doesn't the force of the one-point argument depend, many people say, on limiting consideration to monocular vision? In any case, didn't Charles Wheatstone's invention of the stereoscope show experimentally that there is a means by which we can see distance of itself and immediately; that visual experience, unlike olfactory experience, has an inherent, nonderivative, distance quality? For Wheatstone, with his invention of the stereoscope, demonstrated beyond doubt that binocular disparity, the difference in the images of a scene cast on the retinas of our two eyes, can give rise to a perception of depth.

We now know that when our eyes converge to fixate on a point in space, the light from the point will strike geometrically similar, corresponding

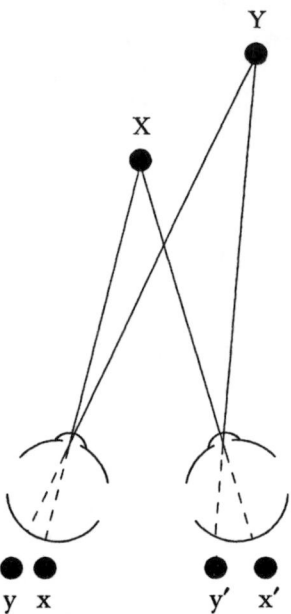

Figure 1.2   *Binocular retinal disparity. Points at different distances from the observer project images with different amounts of separation on each retina.*

points on both retinas. But due to the spatial separation of our eyes, light from points in front or behind the plane of the focal point will strike non-corresponding retinal locations. Figure 1.2 illustrates the situation. The distances between the images of X and Y will not be the same on both retinas, for yx < y′x′. With eyes focused on X, x and x′ will be corresponding points, but y and y′ will not. We can readily notice the effect of this stimulus difference by alternately opening and closing each eye. The visual experience of the left eye is not the same as that of the right. Relative retinal disparity is a measure of the degree of this non-correspondence. If X is kept at a constant distance, the relative retinal disparity will increase or decrease as Y moves closer to or farther away from X. What Wheatstone's stereoscope dramatically showed was that such disparity is actually used by our visual system to give visual experience a pronounced impression of three-dimensional voluminousness. Anyone who has viewed properly prepared photographs through a stereoscope will tell you that the phenomenal effect is powerful and unmistakable.

In the last 50 years such findings have become, perhaps, the most frequently cited empirical results to which philosophers have turned in support of their criticisms of Berkeley. Russell, for example, states outright that "Berkeley's theory of vision according to which everything looks flat, is disproved by the stereoscope."[45] Donagan and Pitcher, after offering sympathetic readings of Berkeley's project, maintain that had Berkeley been aware of the facts about disparity and the stereoscope, he would (or should) have altered his claims about distance perception, and more recent papers have echoed this criticism.[46]

Now it is difficult to be sure just what Berkeley's response to Wheatstone's discovery would have been, since his only discussion of the effects of using two eyes is restricted to his account of convergence. Interestingly too, Berkeley does not treat at all a related problem about binocular vision, a problem that was of major concern to theorists then and now — namely, "How is it that we do not see double, given that each eye can provide its own separate visual experience of the scene?" Nevertheless, I believe that criticisms of Berkeley that cite disparity and the stereoscope tend to run together several historical and empirical issues that should be kept apart. In addition, the assumptions underlying these criticisms often rest on a misunderstanding of crucial aspects of the problem of distance vision, features that must be dealt with if we are to have a coherent theory of our ability to determine distance by sight.

Before examining these issues in more detail, three preliminary remarks are in order. First, it would seem entirely unlikely that Berkeley was unaware of the commonly known fact that distance perception improves and that our experience may seem phenomenally more full-bodied or voluminous with two eyes than with one. Second, we do perceive distance, although not as adequately, when we look with a single eye, and the world viewed monocularly does not appear flat. Does the critic, then, who takes the evidence concerning binocular vision as crucial mean to allow that Berkeley is right about single-eyed vision, or at least allow that the data on monocular vision are compatible with Berkeley's thesis?[47] Finally, and most important, citing Wheatstone's work as an obvious counterexample to Berkeley is historically problematic. Wheatstone's work was done in the mid-1800s, but motor theories remained prominent well beyond that time. Moreover, such criticisms of Berkeley leave unexplained and puzzling why people like Helmholtz, Wundt, Mill, Sully, to an extent Wheatstone himself, and others responded to these stereoscope discoveries in just the opposite fashion. They understood the findings, if anything, to support a Berkeleian position.

A "Berkeleian" Approach to Disparity

Since Berkeley did not write specifically about binocular disparity, we can only speculate as to how he might have handled the issue. It seems reasonable to assume that Berkeley knew that our eyes receive different images when we view objects that are at different distances, but he did not take this, in itself, as a challenge to his position. If subsequent treatment of disparity in the theory of vision is to be a guide, it suggests that a Berkeleian analysis of the phenomena would take the following line. Each eye receives a projection of light from the scene, in accordance with the principles stated in the one-point argument. The horizontal separation between our eyes means, however, that each eye experiences the world from a slightly different vantage point. These visual image differences provide information as to the spatial arrangement of the environment. So if we learn how to interpret the spatial significance of disparity, it can serve as an additional, powerful cue to the third dimension.

On Berkeleian grounds, it might be expected, then, that we would report that real-life binocular vision or prepared stereoscopic pictures containing, as they do, disparity cues give a more pronounced experience of depth than monocular sight. The more cues available, the more easily and firmly do we read through and assign depth significance to our experience. A picture with shading and interposition cues looks more three-dimensional than one that depends solely on perspective. Similarly, disparity data, when "understood," should serve to enhance depth interpretations. If binocular disparity is conceived of in this way, as being a cue to spatial layout, it might not seem, right off, to pose any new difficulty to Berkeley's position, over and above the qualms one may have with the cue model in general.[48]

Immediacy and Binocular Vision

Still, the critic might maintain that this is where Berkeley and his followers go wrong. Disparity should not really be thought of as a cue like other indicators of space. Disparity provides us with a means of seeing distance immediately. Anyone who has looked through a stereoscope can appreciate this face. But just what is this fact we are being asked to appreciate? And is it the case that any student of vision who pays appropriate attention to the stereoscopic demonstrations of Wheatstone will abandon the claim that distance perception is not immediate? Well, as a matter of historical fact, we have already noted that the answer to this latter question is "no." Both prior and subsequent to Wheatstone's work, there was a good deal of debate over whether the processes underlying binocular vision were organic or psychic in nature. A brief sketch of what some of these alternatives are like is instructive.[49]

Consider, first, the problem of explaining why it is that we do not see double when using both eyes. According to one theory, variations of which can be found in Galen, Descartes, Newton, and others, the difficulty is resolved by a simple physiological account of the arrangement of our visual system. The nerve projections from corresponding retinal points, it is claimed, come together and merge. Stimuli striking corresponding retinal locations thus meet and fuse into a single neural impulse, which triggers only a single sensation. We do not experience double vision, since we do not have two sensations to start with. Single vision is explained in entirely physiological terms, requiring no appeal to learning, association, or other mental processing.

The alternative approach to single vision denies that a simple peripheral physiological fusion takes place. Rather, it allows that there is a remaining sensory representation of the separate retinal images. On one version of the story, single vision is achieved by suppressing one of the two sensations. We pay attention to the experience of only one eye at a time, perhaps shifting back and forth between the two. On another account, the two sensations are combined into a single experience, which then becomes the focus of attention. This sort of fusion is a two-step process requiring mental activity to unite the separate sensations. The single unified visual experience is not an immediate product of sense.

Variations of, and alternatives to, both these approaches have been explored, and controversies still abound.[50] Nevertheless, what should be clear is that appreciation of the importance of disparity does not show that it is unnecessary to postulate psychic processes in dealing with the problem of single vision. Indeed, the opposite might seem to be the case. Disparity further complicates matters for the non-psychological, organic approach. As long as our visual system has only to bring together corresponding points, a relatively simple story of how we are "wired," so that the neuronal projections of these points merge, will do the trick. Once we have to cope with the fact that objects not on the fixation plane project onto non-corresponding retinal points, the problem of single vision becomes that much harder to resolve. For non-corresponding points will not come together organically on this simple physiological model. So the existence of disparity only makes the task more difficult for an immediate, neurological treatment of single vision.

The related problem, explaining how our visual system makes use of disparity in perceiving depth, has also received a range of solutions.[51] Again, some theorists have opted for seemingly noncognitive physiological models, while others have favored postulating intermediate steps of mental processing. For example, a theory often said to originate with Kepler had it that the visual system projects out along lines of sight from the two images and locates the source of the images at the intersection of these lines in space. On this model the effects of disparity depend on geometric processing. Berkeley, it will be recalled, argued that this type of model was not psychologically real. Another popular theory, later discredited, sought to account for the effects of disparity simply in terms of convergence. Our eyes rapidly shift from converging on one item to converging on another, and such convergence data are used to determine depth arrangements.

An alternative, more recent solution, the projective field model, turns the Kepler idea inside out. It maintains that the neural projections from points on our retinas do not fuse at a single point, but form a three-dimensional array of intersecting points; thus fusion can take place at differing neural intersections (see figure 1.3). The spatial organization of this neurological array is taken to be isomorphic to that of environmental space. Depending on how this model is fleshed out, it may be thought to provide a noncognitive solution to both the double-image problem and the use of disparity in space perception. The stimuli fuse before triggering any visual experience, and we have a three-dimensional copy of the world mapped directly onto our brain tissue.

Now all these theories of single vision and binocular space perception have their shortcomings, and no totally satisfactory account is at hand.[52] Since, in addition, Berkeley does not discuss the topic at all, it would be pointless to argue about exactly how well or how poorly, and along which dimension, the ultimately correct answer might jibe with his approach. What I hope has emerged from this brief review, however, is that the immediate/non-immediate issue, as it arises in studies of binocular vision, has been largely conceived of as an empirical question about the nature of processing, and, like the debates over neutral color, color contrast, and size perception, is at some remove from philosophical controversies over incorrigibility, appearance/reality distinctions, and so forth. Furthermore,

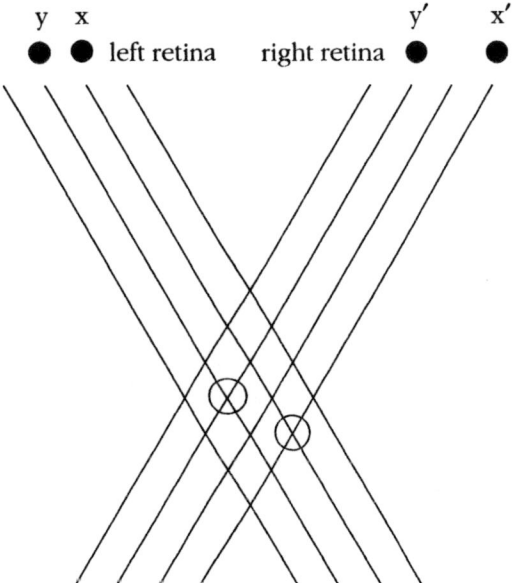

y   x   y'   x'
● ● left retina   right retina ●   ●

Figure 1.3   *The projective field model. The neural projections from the retinas form*
an array that allows fusion to take place at various neural intersections.

it is historically inaccurate to cite the stereoscope as an obvious refutation
of the claim that distance perception is not immediate.

Helmholtz, for example, was well aware of the stereoscope experiments; but he thought that the data indicated the important effects of
learning and so supported a nonorganic model. In the *Physiological Optics*
he concludes a more than 100-page review of the evidence with the claim
that "These experiments show . . . the content of each separate field comes
to consciousness without being fused with that of the other field by
means of organic mechanisms; and that, therefore, the fusion of the two
fields in one common image, when it does occur, is a psychic act."[53]
Similarly, Wilhelm Wundt in his account of the new stereoscope experiments concludes that they show that "There can be no doubt that the
fusion of the two visual images is the result of an act of mental association" and that, as is the case with monocular vision, "in the binocular idea
of depth it is sensations of movement which furnish our primary measures
of spatial distance."[54]

Sully, then, could accurately report in 1878 that the arguments of the
Berkeleians were "aided by experiments of Wheatstone and others." For

not only did these studies not demonstrate that distance was immediate, they were widely taken as a strike against various of Berkeley's competitors. They were thought to run counter to nativist and organic accounts of single vision and to favor models that postulated the need for learning and mental activity to bring together the disparate images. Most significantly, they were thought to undermine the position of Berkeley's major opponents, the "Kantians" or intuitionists. People had long known that our two eyes receive different images. The import of Wheatstone's discovery was that it showed that this disparity was an effective stimulus or cue for depth perception. Locating such an external physical base for depth phenomena meant that it was possible and reasonable to explain depth perception as dependent on *sensory* apprehension. If, as Wheatstone demonstrated, disparity was an actual stimulus for depth perception, it was that much less plausible to assume that spatiality was a non-sensory, a priori imposition of mind. The discovery of the stereoscope "made the dogma of an innate intuition of space – of space as an inner condition of all experience – less likely than ever before."[55]

I believe that the failure of many commentators to appreciate these responses to Wheatstone's work may stem in part from their placing too much emphasis on the indeterminateness aspects of the one-point argument. They are impressed by the fact that with binocular vision there is a *visual* source of information regarding spatial relations. Differences in the spatial separation between objects get reflected in the retinal stimulus as different amounts of disparity. The one-point argument then seems to lose its force, since there is an effective stimulus in the retinal image that varies directly with arrangements in space. But, as I have stressed, stimulus ambiguity is not the primary basis for claiming that distance is not directly represented on the retina and not immediately sensed by sight.

Disparity and the Voluminousness of Visual Space

Even if the stereoscope demonstrations do not entail that distance perception is immediate, does not the voluminous experience that we get when looking through these devices refute Berkeley's additional claim that vision lacks inherent spatiality? Don't stereoscopic phenomena show unmistakably that distance is perceptible by sight? The answer to these questions is also "no." First, we have seen that Berkeley never claimed that our visual sensations were flat; nor did he deny that we would report our visual experience as seemingly three-dimensional. Second, although disparity may serve to provide information about spatial relationships, it does not overturn the basic thrust of the one-point argument. Line-of-sight distances to or between points in space are not *in and of themselves* displayed in the stimulus array. Use of two eyes does not alter the fact that when the three-dimensional world is mapped onto our two-dimensional retinas, nothing directly (re)presents such distances. So it should not be surprising that Wheatstone's stereoscope demonstrations were not assumed to preclude derivative, motor theories of distance perception.

Still, I believe that there is a deeper issue underlying this dimensionality of vision issue that has not as yet been adequately explored, an issue that it is important to examine if we are to understand more fully the problem of distance perception. For if we look closely at our initial question – "What is it to have an idea or evaluation of distance?" – and the related question – "What is it to be a distance-perceiver?" – it is not all that apparent that many of the debates over the fullness or voluminousness of our visual experience are as relevant to these questions as the discussions make them out to be.

To begin with, we have already noted that if we close one eye, our phenomenal experience may lose some of its 3D-ness and our ability to correctly evaluate distance may decline somewhat, yet that, whatever the "flattening" of our visual experience amounts to, we continue to see objects in space and at distances from us. With one-eyed persons or with animals whose two eyes are positioned so that they do not see overlapping scenes with both eyes, there will be no disparity information. We may not have a good grasp of how voluminous their experience is, "what it's like" when they see, but there may be good reason to claim that they perceive distance. As Berkeley would argue, we key our judgment to the organism's ability to use its visual system to guide its activities. What counts is not the phenomenal character of the visual experience, but the organism's ability to read through the experience and come away with its significance for movement.

Next, if by distance one means the metrical distance of an object from the perceiver, what is called the "absolute distance," then there is a sense in which the perceptual appreciation of this spatial property may be distinct from the quality of fullness we report our phenomenal experience as having. Let me try to spell this out. Whether I am looking at my hand, the table across the room, or the moon high in the night sky, I may describe my phenomenal experience as possessing a three-dimensional, non-flat quality to it. In each case, my experience seems more like it is when looking through a stereoscope than when viewing an ordinary single photograph. My evaluations of the absolute distances which these "voluminous" experiences reflect, however, differ greatly. But it is not obvious in what way my phenomenal field is to be thought of as flatter or less three-dimensional when observing my hand than when observing the table or the moon. Just as our phenomenal visual field is no wider (in Berkeley's sense, contains no more minimum visibilia) when we look at an entire mountain range than when we entirely fill our field with a view of the side of a barn, so it is no "deeper" or more "spacious" when viewing distant objects than when viewing those nearby. We might talk appropriately of a change in the overall size of our phenomenal field were we to close one eye or suffer damage to part of our retina. In such cases our experiential field might be said actually to shrink and contain fewer minimum visibilia. This sort of diminution is not what happens, though, when we shift from viewing the distant and wide to observing the near and narrow. It would not seem to make much sense to think of our phenomenal field itself as expanding or contracting in this manner in correspondence to perceived distance or width. Our visual experiences might then be understood as having the same phenomenal fullness and width while signifying vastly different distances and lateral dimensions.

Another way to appreciate this sort of uncoupling of voluminousness from distance is to consider briefly what happens when we look through a stereoscope. If the pictures are properly prepared, our visual experience will have a three-dimensional fullness no less if the scene is of a table across the room than if it is a mountain across the bay. At the same time, talk of our experience of absolute distance from us to either the nearest or most distant object portrayed will seem otiose. Our voluminous phenomenal field does not have a definite quality of distance from us to the objects pictured in it. Furthermore, if the objects and scene displayed have no familiar size or standard proportions, perception of the absolute spatial properties of the depicted items may also appear indeterminate. If we look at stereoscopically prepared views of an undifferentiated sphere, the experience will be 3D-like. The object will appear as a sphere not a circle; the surface of the sphere will seem to curve away in depth. But if we now ask how far it looks from the front to the furthest visible point on the sphere, any very specific answer can feel forced and somewhat unnatural. If we now fill in the picture with additional markings — for example, giving the sphere the distinct color and texture of a cantaloupe

– then the depth relations may begin to look to us more determinate, in the range of 5 inches. Were we to provide instead a different context, have the sphere serve to support a circus elephant, the very same sphere may again take on a more definitive appearance of absolute depth, this time closer to 5 feet than 5 inches.

That there is some uncoupling of the fullness that retinal disparity contributes from our perception of absolute distance and depth should not be unexpected, given the optics of the situation. For retinal disparity, by itself, cannot provide information about the absolute distance of the object from the viewer. Nor, independent of some means of evaluating absolute distance, can it provide a measure of the absolute depth between two objects or between the front and back of a solid object. The reason is that the amount of retinal disparity is a function of both the depth relations and absolute distance.[56] Two points close to each other in depth but near the viewer, may project images with the same amount of disparity as two points widely separated but further away. Similarly, if the spatial separation between the points X and Y in figure 1.2 is kept constant, while their absolute distance from the perceiver changes, the amount of disparity will vary. So disparity differences, by themselves, cannot tell us how far we are from an object; nor can they tell us which of two pairs of objects are closer together in space. Disparity information may serve to recover absolute spatial depth only when conjoined with some measure of distance to scale the significance of the disparity. Thus, the uncoupling and indeterminateness of spatial qualities, which we experience when employing certain optical devices that eliminate distance cues, is what one might expect in light of the inability of disparity alone to provide a basis for evaluating absolute distance and depth.

The Problem of Absolute Distance

The geometrical features of the projection of light that prevent retinal disparity from providing independent information of absolute distance is, moreover, not unique to this cue. It has been long recognized that the standardly cited pictorial cues cannot indicate absolute spatial measures. For example, interposition, the overlap of one object so as to occlude light from another, may serve to indicate that one object is in front of the other, but not how far either of them is from the viewer or from the other. The situation is similar with perspective, height in field, and so on.

This inability of pictorial cues to provide independent information about absolute distance is, of course, the other side of the geometrical considerations that underwrite the one-point argument. Absolute spatial differences may project spatially identical retinal images, and hence the geometrically based pictorial cues will be identical. Use of these cues to determine distance would seem to require additional assumptions or supplemental information. Of the traditional cues, blur and the nonvisual oculomotor cues of convergence and accommodation vary directly with absolute distance. It is not surprising that Berkeley and other theorists would have paid them special attention. What Berkeley wanted to explain was our ability to locate objects in space, to place them at particular distances; but, given the optics of the situation, static visual stimuli were not sufficient to do the job.

What became clearer with later work in the study of vision was that the practice of considering only static sources of information was unnecessarily restrictive. An organism that can move about has a means of enriching the information from geometrical cues by taking into account the patterns of image change that accompany movement. For example, although simple retinal size is no indicator of distance, change of size as we move about is. If we take a step forward, the image projected by an object 4 feet away will become considerably bigger; whereas if the object was originally 20 feet away, the change in proportional image size will be much less. Such differences in rate of change, or ratios, of image size vary directly with absolute distance. Correlates of many of the other static cues can be found that likewise take on new spatial significance when coupled with motion. In recent years, Gibson and his associates have argued that these changes in the flow of optical patterns are crucial to overcoming the inadequacies and inherent ambiguities of the pictorial cues, and they have done much to explore this source of information. The actual importance of all these transformation patterns to distance perception, however, remains a matter of some dispute.[57]

Berkeley, I believe, would have found nothing to get upset about in admitting that static cues can be supplemented with information from patterns of movement-induced image changes associated with distance. The importance of motion for the acquisition and determination of distance ideas is a major theme of the *New Theory*. But Berkeley's insistence on a crucial role for movement and touch goes beyond merely finding a need to supplement static cues with more dynamic ones. For, as Berkeley saw matters, in order to evaluate absolute distance, it is not enough to have cues that happen to vary directly and unambiguously with distance. In addition, we need to assign specific distance signification to the cues. That the value of some stimulus or sensory property K varies uniformly with increases or decreases in distance does not itself tell how far off in space objects are. To be effective, we need a scheme for assigning absolute distance meaning to the values of K. We must know how much distance corresponds to so much K. An attempt to resolve this sort of problem may be seen to lie at the heart of Berkeley's insistence on the need for a scheme of correlation with motor ideas. And this issue, although it has not received a great deal of attention in discussions of distance perception, is a genuine one.

T. G. R. Bower, a student of Gibson and a theorist popularly associated with pro-innateness, anti-Berkeley claims, is among the researchers sensitive to this calibration issue. As Bower sees it, "Absolute distance is the core problem in distance perception."[58] His reason for this claim is essentially the same as Berkeley's: namely, that in order to survive and thrive in the world, we need absolute distance information. "[I]n many real life situations," Bower says, "we need to know how far away an object is *from us*; the expression of *how far* must serve to control behavior." So, like Berkeley, he concludes, in somewhat more modern words, "the term *absolute distance* serves as shorthand for 'spatial variables translated into a form appropriate for the control of spatial motor movements'."[59]

Bower argues, however, that none of the standard static or dynamic cues, in and of themselves, can provide such absolute information. The pictorial or, as he calls them, "painter's cues," by their very nature, are ambiguous and do not vary with absolute distance. Convergence varies with absolute distance, but Bower notes that the significance of convergence data changes as the perceiver grows.

> Suppose we take an adult with an interocular distance of 6 cm. For this adult a convergence angle of 60° specifies an object 5.2 cms. away . . . but consider this in a developmental perspective . . . an infant's eyes are only half that distance apart. The specification that holds true for an adult [60° = 5.2 cm] would not be true for an infant. . . . If binocular stimulation does specify absolute distance . . . it can only be as a result of a scaled matching or calibration process that imparts the requisite information to the binocular system.[60]

A related problem occurs in using information from optical expansion, the change in size of retinal image as we approach an object or the object approaches us. "The amount of expansion consequent to object movement can specify the position of the object relative to its starting point – but in relative, not absolute terms . . . it does not carry any information about absolute distance to a stationary organism."[61] On the other hand, if we move toward an object, the percentage of expansion will vary directly as a function of the distance to the object. The percentage changes by themselves, however, will not have any absolute distance meaning. "We can make such judgments only if we have some non-visual way of calibrating our movement."[62]

Calibration and Movement

But what might such a scaling be like, and how might such a calibration scheme be instituted? One theory of calibration that is of particular interest here maintains that the required scaling results from correlating visual cues with information derived from movement. This, for example, is Lloyd Kaufman's model of how things might work in the case of the two cues we have just discussed. Consider first the distance information provided by optical expansion.

> Suppose that you are at some distance D from an object and then take a step toward it so that the distance is reduced by the length Δ of one step. . . . If the visual angle [a measure of the size of the retinal image] prior to the step is α_1, [and] after the step α_2. . . . It can be shown that $\alpha_2 / \alpha_1 = D / D - \Delta$. Now, suppose that you register your own locomotion in terms of an internal unit corresponding to the size of your pace. [And] Δ represents one unit of locomotion. Then . . . $\alpha_2 / \alpha_1 = D / D - 1$. It follows . . . that $D = 1 / (1 - \alpha_1 / \alpha_2$ [paces]. [By applying this calibration scheme] distance to the object, expressed in terms of units of locomotion, can be derived from the ratios of angular sizes of an object seen at two different distances . . . merely by taking a step toward an unfamiliar object, it is possible to compute the approximate number of paces that you would need to take in order to reach the object.[63]

Kaufman offers a similar account of how convergence might be scaled for absolute distance.

> [I]f the convergence angle at the greater distance is β_1 the angle after one step is β_2 and the distance is expressed in units of locomotion, then

$\beta_2 / \beta_1 = D / D - 1$. It follows that $D = 1 / (1 - \beta_1 / \beta_2)$ paces. Therefore, as in the case of image size, convergence can be calibrated to represent distance merely by moving toward (or away from) an object. The resulting changes in convergence represent distance expressed as units of locomotion.[64]

Now Kaufman admits that the specific calibration schemes he postulates are mere speculation. The plausibility of the claim that vision is in some way scaled in terms of movement is enhanced, though, when one considers the lack of an alternative basis, and that some motor scheme is necessary, in any case, if the organism is to use vision to guide its getting about in the world. Kaufman and Bower indicate that a further consequence of these considerations is that such a scaling matrix will not be innately fixed, since it will depend on the actual size of the inter-ocular separation, the size of one's pace, arm span, and other bodily dimensions. These features change considerably as the child develops. So it would seem that there must be provision for updating the calibration scheme.[65]

Summary Psychological Statement

But if absolute distance is a core problem of visual perception, and if its solution lies in motor correlations, then important aspects of Berkeley's position may remain on firmer scientific ground than is often supposed. For the claim that the distance meaning of visual experience is derivative, that vision must be scaled, and that this calibration is in units of motion constitute the main theses of Berkeley's account of distance perception. Berkeley, as we have seen, accepted as established the claim that distance perception is not immediate. This was agreed by all. In his criticism of the optic writers, he sought to show that we did not acquire distance ideas from vision with the added help of reason. And in his later discussion of his thought experiment concerning the spirit with only a visual sense, Berkeley went on to argue that distance could not be constructed out of sets or series of visual experiences alone. Visual experience could obtain spatial meaning only by being correlated with movement.

Berkeley assumed, perhaps at the time not implausibly, that if visual distance perception depended on a correlation with experience from an entirely different sense modality, a correlation not bridged by either an a priori idea of reason or a shared sensory quality, then the initial calibration must be learned. As Mill was later to argue, this conclusion does not follow. The correlation could be wired in, even if there is no abstract or common idea to link the senses and the connection is purely "accidental."[66] The experience that gives rise to the correlation could be that of our ancestors, passed on to us as part of our biological inheritance. Nonetheless, the tradition of the Berkeleian school was anti-nativist, and the learned versus innate split has been a major battleground in visual science ever since.

Given that the calibration scheme we standardly acquire is not logically necessary, Berkeley further speculated that we should have the capacity to learn alternative schemes. Were our environment or peripheral visual system to change, we should be able to adjust once we have enough data to re-correlate. (Some such lability would, in fact, be required if Kaufman and Bower are right about the need to recalibrate as we grow.) This Berkeleian lability thesis served as a major inspiration for the pioneering work of G. M. Stratton and the subsequent extensive psychological experimentation on our ability to adapt to distorting prisms. When we go around wearing distorting prisms, our standard correlation schemes are no longer adequate. The question is whether we have the capacity to adjust to the new conditions. Berkeley's speculation, that we do have this adaptability, seems consonant with much, but by no means all, of the empirical evidence available.[67]

If, as Berkeley believed, seeing distance depends on learned, non-necessary correlations, it is clear why he would assume that a man born blind and subsequently acquiring sight would not be able, at first, to assess distance visually. Moreover, we can give some empirical sense to the idea that such a man might initially claim to experience the world as "in his mind."[68] For, lacking a scheme of calibration, his visual experiences would have no specific distance significance. They would have no inherent spatial meaning. Berkeley's thought experiment concerning the perceptual incapacities of the disembodied spirit might be given a similar empirical fleshing-out. In this case, the issue is not whether distance perception is innate. The spirit has lots of visual experience and has had time to learn. What the spirit lacks is the requisite tangible sense experience that gives visual experience spatial meaning. Without a calibration scheme, the spirit's visual sensations, although they may be qualitatively the same as our own, would lack distance significance. While it is not possible to test this claim with scientific experiments on spirits, there is some empirical work that might be thought to bear on Berkeley's position here. It has been claimed, for example, that animals that are passively moved, and so have visual experience without feedback from self-initiated locomotion, do not develop normal spatial perception. It is also claimed that people who are passively moved do not adapt to distorting prisms.[69]

These calibration and scaling considerations can now be related back to what I have said is a behaviorist strand in Berkeley's analysis. What it means to be a visual perceiver of distance is, first and foremost, that our visual experience has locomotive significance for us. As Bower puts it, "When speaking of the problem of absolute distance, it is this translation from sensory to motor that I am referring to. If an organism displays behavior that is appropriate to the distance of objects, . . . then I would say the organism is responding to absolute distance." In turn, the crucial test for distance perception will be motor activities. "Obviously," Bower says, "the only acceptable indicators of this capacity are spatial behaviors – behaviors that are *necessarily* adjusted in space."[70] But, as we have seen, Berkeley is arguing for more than a methodological claim that we must rely on behavioral evidence in assessing people's perception, because we have no access to their conscious experiences. It is not just that behavior provides the ultimate test for distance perception; rather, for Berkeley, as in Kaufman's model, visual experience gains its distance significance via a scheme of motor calibration.

We may reasonably guess that, in his day, Berkeley would have had qualms about taking scaling formulas like those Kaufman proposes as representing the actual processes that go on in attaining and applying the correlation schemes. Berkeley would probably have found claims about explicit calculations according to mathematical formulas too "intellectualized" an explanation of what takes place. He would have thought that this model, like the optic writers' model, is not psychologically real. Berkeley's own account of the calibration processes appealed only to learning and association. But then again Kaufman too has reservations about how literally his model should be read. He says, for example, in discussing his calibration scheme for optical expansion, that "There is no evidence that such a process actually takes place. However, some such process must exist or else it would be impossible for us to perceive absolute distance to any object, whether near or far."[71] But he leaves vague how to construe the claim that "some such process" does exist.

Today, of course, with our growing readiness to acknowledge that complex calculations can be done by non-sentient machines, many of Berkeley's aversions to postulating explicit underlying computations appear old-fashioned. At the same time, his questioning of the relationship between formal specifications of a task and psychologically real models of processing remains pertinent. Several of these issues are explored in more detail in the following chapters.

Precisely where Berkeley would come out in these debates, were he alive today, seems to me to be a matter of idle speculation. Although I have mentioned a good deal of contemporary work in this chapter, I see little point in trying to make Berkeley into something he was not, a twentieth-century philosopher and psychologist. I have included this more modern material, along with the earlier work of Helmholtz, James, and others, because I believe it enables us to see better where Berkeley's work fits into the history of the science of vision. In turn, this should enable us to understand better Berkeley's own claims and to see why they had the impact they did. I also think that placing Berkeley in this scientific context can aid our understanding of various of his more philosophical theses. I have briefly noted some of these implications in my discussion of the immediate/non-immediate distinction, and now wish to add, even more sketchily, a few additional remarks on this subject.[72]

Conclusion

I earlier claimed that the immediate/non-immediate dichotomy, as it occurs in empirical hypotheses about visual processes, does not fit well with several of the epistemological distinctions with which it has been associated. It is also unclear that Berkeley's agreeing that visual distance perception is not immediate plays an important role in his own metaphysical idealistic doctrines. Berkeley says this straight out. "But allowing that distance was truly and immediately perceived by the mind, yet it would not thence follow it existed out of the mind. For whatever is immediately perceived is an idea: and can any *idea* exist out of the mind?"[73] Immediate ideas being, by definition, ideas of sense are a paradigm case of ideas whose properties are dependent upon us and the nature of our sensory systems. If distance were like color, a direct quality of visual experience, it might be easier to convince people that such ideas are perceiver-dependent. In some ways distance becomes more of a problem for Berkeley's metaphysical theories when it is conceived of as non-immediate and when the question of the relationship among the senses is taken seriously. For then it remains to be explained how we do in fact acquire such a non-immediate idea of distance, and the possibility arises that the account may be one that makes it independent of sense. It is this latter possibility that Berkeley wants to rule out. Central to Berkeley's metaphysical doctrines is his denial that there are any meaningful abstract ideas. An idea of distance not reduced to sensory terms would be just such an idea. What is pivotal in the *New Theory* is not the argument that distance perception is not immediate but the challenge to views that would go against his empiricism and his anti-abstractionism. The two popular positions that Berkeley thought conflicted with his own principles were the optic writers' claim that we could derive distance ideas via reason and the claim that we have some sort of abstract idea of space that is shared by touch and sight experience. Berkeley therefore devotes most of his critical efforts in the *New Theory* to overturning these theories. It would, moreover, be highly inappropriate for him to attempt to get much metaphysical mileage from the mere claim that distance perception is not immediate, since in the *New Theory* he allows that it is. Distance is immediately perceived by touch.

Thus Berkeley's constructive task in the *New Theory* was to devise an alternative theory of vision that would be compatible with his epistemological and metaphysical convictions, a theory that would be empirically adequate — could account for the facts of visual space perception as well as explain the close relationship between sight and touch — while not presupposing an abstract notion of space. Berkeley thought he had accomplished this by making the spatial significance of visual experience a function of contingently associated tangible ideas. In the *New Theory* he elaborated this thesis with respect to a full range of problems in space perception. In addition to distance, these included magnitude, orientation, direction, motion, and shape. In each of these areas the *New Theory* made its mark. It helped set in motion a scientific research program that influenced the study of vision for a long time after.

In this chapter I have attempted to describe a portion of this history and have primarily emphasized the positive aspects of the story. I do not mean to suggest by this somewhat one-sided treatment that the *New Theory* is error-free, that Berkeley is always clear and consistent, that later research has supported each of his major theses, or that most of the interesting results in the theory of space perception were prefigured in his *New Theory*. I do believe, however, that Berkeley's central claim concerning the derivative nature of the spatial features of visual experience was historically important. And, I believe, it may be theoretically important as well. For, if Berkeley was on the right track about the role of motor calibration, then, as Kaufman concludes, it means that "perceptual space . . . is scaled in terms of locomotion. [And] this . . . has profound implications for any theory of perception . . . [especially] how the senses work together."[74]

Notes

1   John Stuart Mill, "Bailey on Berkeley's Theory of Vision," in *Dissertations and Discussions*, vol. 2 (Haskell House Publications, New York, 1973), p. 84.

2   Thomas Abbott, *Sight and Touch: An Attempt to Disprove the Received (or Berkeleian) Theory of Vision* (Longman, Green, Longman, Roberts, and Green, London, 1964), p. 1.

3   Alan Donagan, "Berkeley's Theory of the Immediate Objects of Vision," in *Studies in Perception*, ed. P. Machamer and R. Turnbull (Ohio State University Press, Columbus, 1978), p. 332.

4   Julian Hochberg, *Perception* (Prentice-Hall, Englewood Cliffs, N.J., 1965), p. 43.

5   George Pitcher, *Berkeley* (Routledge and Kegan Paul, London, 1977), p. 97.

6   Hermann von Helmholtz, *Treatise on Physiological Optics*, vol. 3, ed. James Southall (Dover, New York, 1950), p. 6.

7   Bertrand Russell, *Human Knowledge: Its Scope and Limits* (Simon and Schuster, New York, 1964), p. 51.

8   James Sully, "The Question of Visual Perception in Germany, I," *Mind*, 9 (1878), p. 1.

9   See Margaret Atherton, *Berkeley's Revolution in Vision* (Cornell University Press, Ithaca, N.Y., 1990) for a more detailed examination of this topic.

10   See, e.g., Donagan, "Berkeley's Theory"; Pitcher, *Berkeley*; D. M. Armstrong, *Berkeley's Theory of Vision* (Melbourne University Press, Melbourne, 1960); or the influential analysis of J. L. Austin, *Sense and Sensibilia* (Oxford University Press, Oxford, 1964).

11   A review of the psychological literature would reveal that the notion of "distance perception" has been and continues to be interpreted, used, and measured in incompatible ways by vision theorists. Running together these different construals has been a source of much confusion in discussions of distance perception.

12   René Descartes, *Le Monde, ou Traité de la lumière*, tr. Michael Mahoney (Arabis Books, New York, 1979), ch. 1, and John Locke, *An Essay Concerning Human Understanding*, ed. Peter Nidditch (Clarendon Press, Oxford, 1975), bk II, ch. ix, sect. 9.

13   See esp. the *New Theory*, sect. 145 or 159, or Berkeley's *The Theory of Vision or Visual Language Vindicated*, sect. 52; but the general idea permeates both works.

14   In an illuminating paper, "The sensory Core and the Medieval Foundations of Early Modern Perceptual Theory", *Isis*, 70 (1979), pp. 363–84, Gary Hatfield and William Epstein trace the development of this distinction and the related concept of a sensory core from ancient times up to Berkeley. It should be noted that, in laying out this issue, I have been using the phrase "mental processing" broadly to include any activity in which one ideational element plays a role in bringing to mind another, whether the activity be attributed to the doings of the intellect, the imagination, or some other faculty. One also finds distinctions in the literature between processes of suggestion and those of inference, between innate and acquired processes, etc. These classifications and the relationships assumed to hold among them figure differently for different writers and affect how each conceives of and talks about particular processes. Although being clear about these distinctions is crucial for understanding certain issues in the theory of vision, I believe it is not necessary to consider them in detail here. These issues loom large in chapters 3 and 4.

15   See esp. vol. 3, sect. 26, "Concerning the Perceptions in General." Although Helmholtz calls the underlying processes of his model cases of "unconscious inference," his explicit characterization of them would seem to fit Berkeley's category of processes of suggestion. Chapter 3 takes up this issue in more detail.

Throughout these essays I stress important similarities between Berkeley's and Helmholtz's positions, but emphasizing such resemblances is by no means unique to me. This is not to overlook significant disagreements between their positions; nor is it meant to overlook the fact that Helmholtz's elaborate empirical and theoretical studies go way beyond Berkeley's speculations. Moreover, there is a further problem in stressing the commonalities of their views. Helmholtz took pains to trace the historical background of the issues he explores. It may be somewhat surprising, then, to find so little acknowledgment of Berkeley's work in Helmholtz's historical remarks. While I have some thoughts about the influence of Kant's writings and ideas here, I have not been able to come up with a totally satisfactory explanation of this discrepancy.

16   Shimon Ullman, "Against Direct Perception," *Behavioral and Brain Sciences*, 3 (1980), p. 374.

17   See, though, chapters 3 and 4 where I argue that reliance on this sort of dichotomy has largely outlived its usefulness.

18   In Berkeley's terminology, our experience of the square contains more and differently ordered minimum visibilia than our experience of the circle. For

an account of Berkeley's notion of "minimum visibilia," see Atherton, *Berkeley's Revolution in Vision*, pp. 115–17 and 133–5.

19   Irvin Rock, *An Introduction to Perception* (Macmillan, New York, 1975), p. 505.

20   Ibid., p. 506. Rock notes that there are some important differences between the two most popular noncognitive approaches, but they are not crucial for the issue under consideration here.

21   For more on size perception, see chapters 2 and 4.

22   For an account of many of these, see Julian Hochberg, "Perception, I and II," in *Woodworth and Schlossberg's Experimental Psychology*, ed. J. Kling and L. Riggs (Holt, Rinehart and Winston, New York, 1971), pp. 395–550.

23   See G. J. Warnock, *Berkeley* (Penguin, London, 1953), ch. 9. For further discussion, see I. C. Tipton, *Berkeley: The Philosophy of Immaterialism*, (Methuen, London, 1974), pp. 213ff.

24   This would seem to put in question a view of Richard Rorty and others that, historically, incorrigibility has been taken as the mark of the mental. See Richard Rorty, *Philosophy and the Mirror of Nature* (Princeton University Press, Princeton, N.J., 1979), pt. I.

25   Berkeley does not say exactly whom he includes under this label. In the *New Theory* he mentions, among others, the works of I. Barrow, A. Tacquet, W. Molyneux, and J. Wallis. In an appendix to the *New Theory* he explicitly cites Descartes's account of distance. On the basis of remarks in his *Philosophical Commentaries*, there is reason to believe that Malebranche was a main target; but the ideas Berkeley considers were widespread.

26   Berkeley, *New Theory*, Appendix, p. 237. For a more detailed account of the optic writers' position, see Atherton, *Berkeley's Revolution in Vision*.

27   Armstrong, *Berkeley's Theory of Vision*, pp. 20ff., discusses such an objection, and Pitcher, *Berkeley*, p. 22, raises related points.

28   Barrow's case involves the arrangement of a lens or mirror that causes the light rays from a point in space to converge in a way that precludes their being focused as a single point on the retina. According to the geometric formulas employed by the optic writers, the distance calculated on the basis of converging angle data will place the point extremely far, if not infinitely far, away. But the point is not so perceived. Berkeley took this as evidence against the psychological reality of the optic writers' model and in favor of his own account based on experienced visual blur.

29   For more on this issue, see C. M. Turbayne, *The Myth of Metaphor* (University of South Carolina Press, Columbia, 1970), and David Lindberg, *Theories of Vision from Al-Kindi to Kepler* (University of Chicago Press, Chicago, 1976).

30   See, e.g., A. David Kline, "Berkeley, Pitcher and Distance Perception," *International Studies in Philosophy*, 12 (1980), pp. 1–8, and T. G. R. Bower, *Development in Infancy* (W. H. Freeman, San Francisco, 1974), p. 66.

31   Also note that the facts about light that underlie accommodation and convergence may provide unambiguous distance information without at all
implying that distance is immediately seen.

32   See Lindberg, *Theories of Vision*.

33   Rock, *Introduction to Perception*, pp. 79–80.

34   James J. Gibson, "Three Kinds of Distance that can be Seen, or How Bishop
Berkeley Went Wrong," in *Studies in Perception: Festschrift for Fabio Metelli*,
ed. G. Flores D'Arcais (Martello-Guinti, Milan and Florence, 1976), p. 83.

35   This would seem to be a significant break with the optic writers, for whom
the mediate idea of distance was a more abstract representation of space. See
Atherton, *Berkeley's Revolution in Vision*, for a fuller account of this difference.

36   At places Berkeley offers an analogy with our sense of sound.

37   Armstrong, *Berkeley's Theory of Vision*, p. 6.

38   Ibid., p. 5.

39   Berkeley, *New Theory*, sect. 158. See also *Theory of Vision Vindicated*, sect. 46
and 47.

40   Chapter 2 takes up aspects of Berkeley's approach to size.

41   William James, *The Principles of Psychology* (Dover, New York, 1950), vol.
2, p. 272. Whether James and other perceptual psychologists who cite or
appeal to Kant correctly understood the implications of Kant's position
for empirical theories of vision is a real question. See Gary Hatfield, *The
Natural and the Normative* (MIT Press, Cambridge, Mass.,1990), esp. ch. 3,
for the claim that many theorists really misunderstood the empirical implications of Kant's ideas. Moreover, Hatfield argues that Kant's empirical
claims about vision and touch are much like Berkeley's. "[Kant] makes
vision depend upon touch for its ability to perceive objects in depth, thereby
implying the standard Berkeleyan account" (p. 105).

42   James, *Principles of Psychology*, vol. 2, p. 215. Chapter 20 also contains a
short historical review of the competing positions.

43   For a summary of some of these issues, see Sully, "Visual Perception in
Germany, I & II." See Also Helmholtz, *Physiological Optics*, vol. 3, sect. 33.
For more recent surveys, see James J. Gibson, *The Perception of the Visual
World* (Houghton Mifflin, Boston, 1950), ch. 2, and Hatfield, *Natural and
Normative*, ch. 3–5.

44   Hochberg, *Perception*, p. 43.

45   Russell, *Human Knowledge*, p. 51.

46   Donagan, "Berkeley's Theory"; Pitcher, *Berkeley*; and, e.g., Kline, "Berkeley,
Pitcher and Distance Perception." But I have heard the claim widely
repeated by psychologists and philosophers.

47   Also, there are animals that see distance, but whose eyes are so placed that
there is no overlap of their retinal images.

48   Indeed, disparity is standardly treated and talked about as a cue in vision

textbooks. In *Berkeley*, Pitcher argues that it would be a problem for Berkeley to admit disparity as a cue, since we are not consciously aware of the difference between the stimuli to each eye. This criticism seems to me unconvincing. If we close one eye at a time, we do notice a difference in what we see. Many theorists in the Berkeleian tradition took this difference in the experienced sensations to be the basis for disparity phenomena. Again, of course, we may not be aware of or able to report on what is immediately seen in binocular vision, once we come to read through these experiences. See, e.g., Hermann von Helmholtz, "The Recent Progress of the Theory of Vision," in *Helmholtz on Perception: Its Physiology and Development*, ed. Richard Warren and Roslyn Warren (Wiley, New York, 1968), pp. 118ff.

49   See Helmholtz, *Physiological Optics*, vol. 2, pp. 482ff., for a summary of competing early approaches.

50   See Lloyd Kaufman, *Sight and Mind* (Oxford University Press, Oxford, 1974), ch. 8, for a contemporary review of the issues.

51   Ibid.

52   Issues became more complex once it was realized that the visual system must resolve an additional problem before fusion can take place or disparity information can be tapped. The system must decide which points on one retina go together with which points on the other. How, for instance, does the system determine (see Figure 1.2) that x and x' really correspond, rather than x and y'? Until a decision is made about which retinal points go together, not much can be done to unite the retinal images or to use the disparity differences to evaluate space. Consideration of this more modern "correspondence problem" would take us far afield from our study of Berkeleian concerns. The important work of David Marr, *Vision* (W. H. Freeman, San Francisco, 1982), argues for an account that depends on constraints and complex computations.

53   Helmholtz, *Physiological Optics*, vol. 3, p. 499. And in "Recent Progress," Helmholtz introduces his discussion on an even more Berkeleian note: "The invention of the stereoscope . . . made the difficulties and imperfections of the Innate Theory more obvious than before and led to another solution which approached much nearer to the older view. . . . This assumes that none of our sensations give us anything more than 'signs' for external objects and movements and that we can only learn how to interpret these signs by means of experience and practice" (p. 110).

54   Wilhelm Wundt, *Lectures on Human and Animal Psychology*, tr. J. E. Creighton and E. B. Thorndike (Macmillan, New York, 1896), p. 189.

55   Gibson, *Perception of the Visual World*, p. 21.

56   For a survey of this issue, see, Hiroshi One and James Comerford, "Stereoscopic Depth Constancy," in *Stability and Constancy in Visual Perception*, ed. William Epstein (Wiley, New York, 1977), pp. 91–128.

57   See chapter 4 for further discussion of this Gibsonian alternative.

58   Bower, *Development in Infancy*, p. 74.

59   Ibid., pp. 75–6.

60   Ibid., pp. 68–9.

61   Ibid., p. 72.

62   Ibid., p. 71.

63   Lloyd Kaufman, *Perception: The World Transformed* (Oxford University Press, Oxford, 1979), pp. 224ff.

64   Ibid., p. 225.

65   See Claes von Hofsten, "Binocular Convergence as a Determinant of Reaching Behavior in Infancy," *Perception*, 6 (1977), pp. 139–44, for a challenge to some of these assumptions.

66   Mill, "Bailey on Berkeley's Theory of Vision," pp. 96ff. Mill goes on to explain, however, that this sort of innateness is compatible with Berkeley's main ideas about the derivative nature of visual space perception.

67   See Irvin Rock, *The Nature of Perceptual Adaptation* (Basic Books, New York, 1966), and Robert Welch, "Adaptation of Space Perception," in *Handbook of Perception and Human Performance*, vol. 1, ed. K. Boff, L. Kaufman and J. Thomas (Wiley, New York, 1986), ch. 24.

68   Berkeley, *New Theory*, sect. 41.

69   See Richard Held, "Plasticity in Sensory-Motor Systems," in *Perception: Mechanisms and Models*, ed. Richard Held and Whitman Richards (W. H. Freeman, San Francisco, 1972), pp. 327–9. These claims have not gone undisputed; see Robert Welch, *Perceptual Modification: Adapting to Altered Sensory Environments* (Academic Press, New York, 1978).

70   Bower, *Development in Infancy*, p. 76. For a further consideration of the issue, see A. Yonas and H. L. Pick, "An Approach to the Study of Infant Space Perception," in *Infant Perception: From Sensation to Perception*, vol. 2, ed. L. Cohen ans S. Salapatek (Academic Press, New York, 1975), pp. 3–31.

71   Kaufman *Perception*, p. 225.

72   See Atherton, *Berkeley's Revolution in Vision*, for a consideration of many of these issues.

73   Berkeley, *Three Dialogues between Hylas and Philonous*, p. 202.

74   Kaufman, *Perception*, pp. 225–6.

2 Size

In sections 52–87 of *New Theory* Berkeley considers the question of size perception. "[H]ow is it," he asks, "that we perceive by sight the magnitude of objects?"[1] Although these sections raise important issues for the theory of vision, they have received comparatively little examination.[2] In part, this is due to the fact that many commentators assume that the significant philosophical points have already been raised in Berkeley's discussion of distance and that nothing new is to be found these sections. In part, it is also due to a lack of appreciation of major aspects of Berkeley's theoretical and empirical claims and how they fit in with early and current work on size perception. Some of the more recent neglect of Berkeley's position, I think, may be traced to a very popular paper by Lloyd Kaufman and Irvin Rock which appeared in *Scientific American*.[3] In this paper, Kaufman and Rock claimed to have refuted Berkeley's own account of the moon (size) illusion, while showing that the taking-account-of-distance model (hereafter the TAD model) of size perception, which Berkeley opposed, is really the correct theory.[4] The Kaufman and Rock paper, however, can prove misleading on a few points. It does not take into consideration Berkeley's main criticism of the TAD model; nor does it deal with one of the problems which Berkeley thought his own account could solve better than the competing TAD theory. More on this later.

What is "the" problem of size perception? The basic issue confronting theories of size perception has continued to be conceptualized along much the same lines as it was in Berkeley's day.[5] While the real, or physical, size of an object is independent of its distance from an observer, the size of the image that the object casts on the retina varies with the distance. Figure 2.1 sets out the problem as it is typically presented in psychological works on size perception. When an object of constant size h is moved

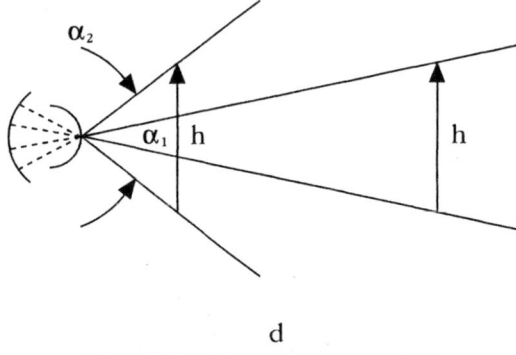

Figure 2.1   *The size of the visual angle, α, of an object of size h varies with the distance d of the object from the observer.*

further from the eye, its retinal image decreases in size. The angle α which the object subtends, the visual angle, is directly correlated with the image size. It is usual practice to talk about the extent of the retinal image in terms of the size of the corresponding visual angle.

The problem of size perception, then, is that of explaining our ability to evaluate magnitude in light of the variability in the size of the visual angles an object can subtend. Now, while this geometrical fact may set the stage for most considerations of size perception, there are several different psychological phenomena that theories of vision have attempted to address. Often the primary focus of attention has been to account for size constancy. Within limits, as we move to or away from an object, the object does not appear to change its size. The book or chair is seen to be of constant size when viewed from 2 feet away or 9 feet across the room. In addition, the more distant chair is perceived to be bigger than the nearby book, even though the sizes of the accompanying retinal images are the reverse. A related, less discussed question concerns our ability to determine the specific or absolute size of an object. We not only see the book as of constant size, but we can tell, more or less, what size it is — that it is about 1 foot long or small enough to pick up with one hand. Still, it is widely acknowledged that our ability to perceive size is often not veridical. Size constancy breaks down in many situations, and our estimates of specific sizes are not very accurate. We are also subject to systematic illusions. Under various circumstances, an object of the same constant physical size will look quite different in magnitude. The moon at its zenith (or, as Berkeley says, at the meridian) looks much smaller than the moon on the horizon, although its size is the same, and the magnitude of the retinal images cast are approximately equal in each case. A full account of size perception should explain these failures of perception as well as our successes. In the *New Theory*, Berkeley attempts to deal with all three of these topics: constancy, specific size, and mistakes or illusions.

It is worth mentioning that there is a good deal of ambiguity, even in the recent psychological literature, concerning the appropriate interpretation and testing of size evaluations. For example, does the concept of "size constancy" refer to the constancy of our determinations of the actual size of physical objects? Or does it refer to the fact that evaluations of phenomenal size are more constant than one might expect, given the variability in the size of the retinal image? There are also problems concerning how to measure these different notions of constancy.[6] Similar conceptual and methodological issues plague other characterizations of the nature of size evaluation. A strength of Berkeley's analysis of magnitude estimation is his attempt to sort out and clarify these matters.

Berkeley on Size

Berkeley's story about size has much in common with his approach to distance, although some of his points are easier and others harder to make here than in the case of distance. One might gloss Berkeley's distance claims in sections 2 and 11 of the *New Theory* with the following claims about size perception. "It is, I think agreed by all that [*magnitude*], of itself and immediately, can not be seen" and "[I]t is plain that [*magnitude*] is in its own nature imperceptible and yet it is perceived by sight." These remarks, too, can be separated into different theses: (1) an account of what it means to have an idea or evaluation of magnitude, (2) the view that the ideas of magnitude gained by sight are not immediate, and (3) the claim that, in and of itself, magnitude is imperceptible by sight.

Claim 2, again seemed obvious to many workers in the field at the time. The size of a physical object does not change as its distance from us varies, although the size of its retinal image, the visual angle, does. Since it was widely assumed that the amount of our sensed visual field (or, in Berkeley's terminology, the number of minimum visibilia sensed) depends on the extent of the retina stimulated, our immediate experiences of an object will vary when it is at different distances from us. A nearby tower will occupy a large portion of our visual field, while the same tower, viewed from half a mile away, will appear as a speck. Our everyday idea of an object's (constant) physical size cannot be identified with each of the distinct visual ideas we *immediately* experience when viewing the object from a variety of distances. Size perception involves a two-step mental process: our immediate sensation, a function of the amount of the retina stimulated, and our idea of a constant physical size that this sensation helps to trigger. According to Berkeley, there is, moreover, no one visual experience that can be singled out as *the* correct or veridical visual idea that goes with a given spatial size.[7]

Berkeley's version of (1) is that what we ordinarily mean by an object's magnitude is its tangible extent, the number of minimal tangibilia we would experience were we to explore the object end to end. Experienced tangible extent of an object does not vary in the way that visual magnitude does. Evaluation of physical size by sight, then, requires that we "read through" our immediate visual sensations to their tangible significance. Because our attention tends to focus on this idea of tangible size, we usually do not pay heed to the fluctuations of our immediate visual experiences. So, within limits, we tend to think that the visual phenomena are themselves more constant than they really are. This is Berkeley's account of our experience of both physical and phenomenal size constancy.

More controversially, Berkeley goes on to maintain that our ideas of visual and tangible magnitude are completely distinct. They are not both instances of some general abstract idea of size, and knowledge or experience of one gives us no purchase on the other. We are mistaken when we think that visual extent shares a common idea of extension with tangible extent. A person who had only visual experience could no more have an understanding of physical size than he or she could have an appreciation of the idea of a lemony taste or an oniony smell. Sight is not the source; nor does it provide the content of our basic ideas of spatial extent. Hence, Berkeley's claim (3), that, strictly speaking, magnitude is imperceptible to sight.

By what means, then, are the magnitudes of objects perceived by sight? For Berkeley, visual extent and familiarity play a role, along with most of the visual and oculomotor cues cited earlier in his account of the perception of distance. We have learned to correlate these cues with "real" or tangible magnitude. What is especially important about Berkeley's model, however, is the way(s) in which it differs from that of the optic writers. The optic writers, too, held that size perception was not immediate;

but they championed a version of the TAD model of size evaluation. According to this theory, we perceive size on the basis of an initial or prior evaluation of distance. Given an appreciation of the visual angle and knowledge of the object's distance, we can geometrically compute its magnitude.

Berkeley agrees with the optic writers that visual size perception is not immediate, but he denies that it involves an initial determination of distance and subsequent computation of magnitude based on this idea of distance. Berkeley offers several reasons for rejecting the TAD model. First, he thinks that introspection does not reveal the existence of processes of calculation involving angles and distances. Allowing, however, for the vagaries of introspection (as discussed in chapter 1), this does not clinch the argument for Berkeley. Second, Berkeley claims that the TAD model cannot account for certain empirical data as well as his theory can. He spends a large part of sections 52–87 elaborating this criticism. In particular, he believes that his own explanation of the moon illusion, one of the most discussed puzzles in vision theory, is better than anything the optic writers have to offer.

Important though, for Berkeley, a complete account of the illusion should include not only an explanation of why the horizon moon looks bigger than the meridian moon, but also an explanation of why the horizon moon itself appears a different size on some occasions than on others. Finally, and I think of most interest, Berkeley raises theoretical and empirical objections to a major feature of the TAD model. Taken literally, the model requires that we make use of our background knowledge and the relevant visual and oculomotor cues to determine an object's distance *prior* to evaluating its size. This distance information, along with knowledge of the visual angle, is needed to compute the magnitude. But, Berkeley argues, there are no good grounds for believing that such an intermediary step of distance evaluation occurs as part of the processes underlying size perception. Instead, he claims that the cues of accommodation, convergence, height in field, interposition, and others are as directly associated with size as they are with distance. There is no more reason to think of them as "distance" cues than to think of them as "size" cues. Magnitude perception is not immediate, it does depend on a prior registration of cues; but it does not depend on a prior evaluation of distance.

I mentioned earlier that Kaufman and Rock claim to have refuted both Berkeley's account of the moon illusion and his critique of the TAD model. Berkeley had maintained that a primary reason for the moon illusion is the presence of atmospheric vapor, or mist, between the observer and the moon when the moon is on the horizon. It is the presence of these vapors, not simply the presence of the terrain, that causes us to see the moon as larger on the horizon. The mist makes the moon appear fainter, and greater faintness is a cue for greater magnitude. Berkeley attached special significance to this cue, because he thought that it also helped to explain why even the horizon moon may look different from one viewing to another. His explanation was that the amount of atmospheric mist on the horizon varies from time to time. Nevertheless, Berkeley explicitly discussed and allowed for the role of many other cues, "any one of which being omitted or varied may suffice to make some alteration in our judgement."[8]

Kaufman and Rock claim that their experiments show that Berkeley was wrong about the significance of mist and wrong in denying the importance of the information that the terrain provides when looking at the horizon moon. On their account, the presence of the terrain causes the moon to be placed at a greater distance on the horizon than when seen at its zenith. Since, on the TAD model, size is computed on the basis of distance and for a given visual angle varies directly with this distance, it follows that the moon should appear larger when it is on the horizon. Two points missing from Kaufman and Rock's article render their remarks about Berkeley somewhat misleading. A major reason for Berkeley emphasizing the role of mist was his concern to explain the differences in perceived size when viewing the horizon moon on separate occasions. This is an issue that Kaufman and Rock do not really address. Clearly, citing the presence of terrain cannot serve to distinguish these cases. Berkeley's deeper complaint against the TAD model, though, was not over which cues are the most prominent; rather, it was over the model's account of the processing that underlies size perception. Berkeley rejected the claim that size perception depends on the prior evaluation of distance. He did not claim that the standard "distance" cues do not play a role in the perception of magnitude. On his own theory they do. What he challenged was the appropriateness of labeling these cues "distance" cues, as opposed to calling them "size" cues. According to Berkeley, the cues serve both functions, and they suggest magnitude and distance evaluations in the same way. This is not merely a terminological quibble. It marks Berkeley's rejection of the TAD model's proposal regarding the processing steps that the visual system actually goes through in determining size. It is to deny the "psychological reality" of a processing stage that incorporates an explicit representation of distance and the use of this measure to then compute magnitude.

Although Berkeley and the optic writers' models make different empirical claims about processing, teasing apart and testing these rival hypotheses is no easy matter. The predicted effects on size perception of manipulating or altering the cues can be much the same on either theory. And debates over these competing accounts of size perception continue.[9] Curiously, Kaufman and Rock point out a difficulty with their own theory that may be seen to favor Berkeley's approach. On their TAD account of the moon illusion, the reason that the moon is said to look bigger on the horizon is that it is mistakenly perceived to be further away than when it is up above. Plugging this larger distance value into the formula we use to compute magnitude yields a larger size evaluation for the horizon moon. A major problem with this explanation, however, is that, if asked to judge the distance of the moon, people tend to maintain that the moon is further away at its zenith than it is on the horizon. Quite understandably, many theorists have taken such distance evaluations to refute the TAD model of the moon illusion. Kaufman and Rock attempt to deal with this seeming contradiction to their theory by arguing that although people do make these distance judgments, these are not the judgments that the visual system relies on in making size determinations. Such conscious distance judgments depend on an added bit of "intellectual" reasoning, over and above the initial verdict that the visual system itself supplies. Kaufman and Rock claim that our visual system really does see the moon as further away on the horizon than when it is up above, and that these distance evaluations are fed into the mechanisms of size perception. The difference between these initial distance measures is what accounts for the size illusion. Kaufman and Rock argue, however, that people then go on to "reason" that since the moon looks bigger on the horizon, it must be closer. It is such rationalizations that subjects report.[10]

In later works, Rock elaborates his own version of this position.[11] He maintains that what gets used in size perception calculation is not the intellectually influenced distance value, but what he calls the "registered distance." Rock waffles somewhat when it comes to spelling out what registered distance amounts to. On one reading, it is an unconscious representation of a specific distance value. Often, though, he talks as if what are registered are only the (distance) cues themselves, and that they directly influence size. But if it is registered cues *about* distance, not a distance value itself, that play a role, it would seem that Rock has gone a long way towards accepting one of Berkeley's central criticisms of the TAD model.

The TAD Model

Sorting out and empirically distinguishing between these two accounts of size perception is, as indicated, a delicate task. It is not obvious, moreover, that either of them is on the right track. Proponents of Gestalt and Gibsonian approaches to spatial perception reject both theories. Nevertheless, over the years the TAD model has had widespread appeal, and its influence remains strong today. In the rest of this chapter I wish to explore some theoretical and technical problems with the TAD model. These difficulties raise questions about both the proper interpretation and the plausibility of the model, once it is more adequately spelled out.

Another look at the geometry of the situation will illustrate the issues most readily (see figure 2.1). For an object of given size h, the size of α varies with the distance d according to the formula $\alpha = h / d$.[12] In turn, the physical size h can be computed from α and d by the equation $h = \alpha \times d$. This formula merely describes the physical facts, however. What the TAD model does, at least in its more modern presentations, is to exploit this mathematical relationship in offering an explanation of the actual processes that underlie size perception. The TAD theorists' proposed psychological correlate of the geometric formula is: perceived size = visual angle × perceived distance, or $H = \alpha \times D$. (I use capital letters to indicate perceived or registered values and lowercase letters for the actual physical values. Often in accounts of the model no distinction is made between α and registered α, and I follow suit)[13]. Our visual system is said to compute size via this "psychologized" formula. Size perception is derived from retinal image size and the distance at which we perceive the object to be. The model gets its name from the claim that the perception of size is in this way based on taking distance into account. But it is perceived or apparent distance, D, not the actual distance, d, that enters into the equation.

The substitution of D for d is required, since the most that the visual system can have as data is its own evaluation of distance, not the actual distance measure. What's more, this shift from d to D is seen as a key to the TAD model's ability to explain various challenging aspects of size perception – in particular, size illusions such as the moon illusion. Similarly, TAD theorists have employed the model to explain the size experiences we have of afterimages. In the case of an afterimage there is no object corresponding to the afterimage that is located at a physical distance d from the perceiver. Subjects report, however, that the apparent size of an afterimage varies directly with the distance of the surface on which it is projected. An afterimage resulting from a retinal stimulus whose visual angle is α will appear greater as the distance D at which it appears to be localized in space increases. The description of this covariance is known as Emmert's law.

As I am using terms, the TAD model differs from and makes a stronger claim than what has been called the "Invariance Hypothesis" (I.H.). The I.H. (in one of its many formulations) says that for a given α, perceived size is proportional to apparent distance; or, more specifically, that there is a unique ratio of H to D corresponding to α. The I.H., on this reading, merely states a correlation. It holds that α and estimates of D and H go together, or are coupled, in a certain way. Emmert's law, understood simply as a description of the phenomenon of afterimages, can be considered a subcase of the I.H. By itself, then, the I.H. does not make any claim about the actual stages of visual processing. The TAD model, on the other hand, involves a claim about these underlying psychological mechanisms. It purports to explain the phenomena that the I.H. (and Emmert's law) claim to describe. Indeed, the I.H. falls out as a necessary consequence of the TAD model. This result is thought by many to be one of the model's great merits.[14] Another attractive feature of the TAD model is its seeming simplicity, the elegant matching of $H = \alpha \times D$ with the geometric facts, as expressed in $h = \alpha \times d$.

With all this going for it, it is not surprising that the TAD model has remained hearty, in spite of numerous attempts to overturn it. Yet, it seems to me that there are some critical problems with the TAD model. And while these problems may not serve outrightly to refute the model, they raise questions both about its correct interpretation and its inherent plausibility. At the same time, several of the issues to be considered here are of a more general nature. They concern basic aspects of the geometry of size evaluation, the distinction between perceived size and distance measures, and the status of the I.H. So although I will set out the discussion in terms of the TAD model, it will be seen that various of the points examined have implications for other views as well.

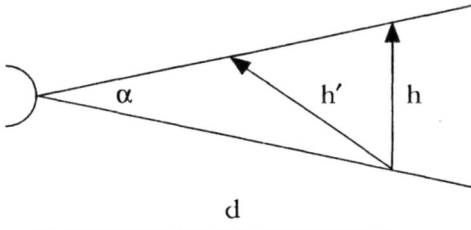

Figure 2.2   h′, *not on the vertical plane perpendicular to the line of sight, poses a problem for the simple characterization of the geometry and perception of size.*

In the standard presentation of the TAD model, as illustrated in figure 2.1, the object whose size is to be determined stands vertically on a plane perpendicular to the line of sight. Our ability to perceive size, however, is not restricted to objects located on such fronto-parallel planes. The world is full of objects or parts of objects lying on planes that are not perpendicular to our line of sight, and we perceive their size too. But when an object is not on this plane, $H = \alpha \times D$ cannot be used to evaluate its magnitude.

Figure 2.2, in which one of the poles tilts toward the observer, illustrates the problem. While there is no difference in either α or d, h′ is bigger than h and may be so perceived.[15] How then is $H = \alpha \times D$ to be used to explain this difference? Moreover, what is to count as the relevant d that D is supposed to measure in estimating h′? The points at the top of the pole are much nearer than those at the bottom, and each point on the pole is at both a different line-of-sight distance and a different ground distance from the observer. There is no one d and corresponding D that will set the significance of α as a whole. Talk of the size or perceived size of the tilted pole as it is at d or D makes little sense, since as a whole it is at no one distance. Stipulating that the distance here is to be understood as the ground distance at the base, where the pole is anchored, will not do alone, since this distance is the same for both the upright and tilted poles. In addition, since most of the everyday objects we see are not themselves directly in touch with the ground, any such notion of "size" would be largely inapplicable to real-life situations. Thus, without some modification, $H = \alpha \times D$ does not provide a basis for explaining the perception of h′ or the difference we may perceive between h′ and h. There is no appropriate single D value to plug into the formula.

Now vision theorists are well aware that, *strictly speaking*, the formula

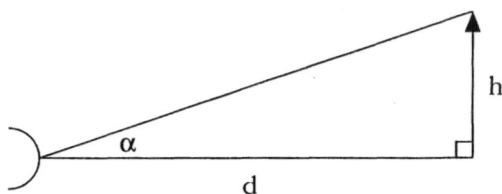

Figure 2.3   *Standard accounts of size estimation based on principles of triangulation strictly hold only for right triangles.*

$H = \alpha \times D$ does not hold for objects not on a fronto-parallel plane. The problem, though, does not get raised, as here, in terms of the lack of a well-motivated notion of "the distance." I think it is very instructive to examine the issue from this perspective. It can help to counter the tendency, especially among TAD adherents, to play down the significance of the difficulties posed for a general theory of size perception. Usually TAD theorists talk as if the formula is approximately right or true under certain idealizations, and maintain that any needed adjustments in the model will leave the overall picture pretty much intact. It is also not uncommon in the literature to find the whole issue sidestepped by the expedient of defining "size" as linear extent on a fronto-parallel plane and "distance" as expanse on a sagittal plane. In turn, it is quite standard in experiments on size perception to test subjects using only two-dimensional objects situated entirely on a fronto-parallel plane. Given these assumptions and practices, the inadequacies of $H = \alpha \times D$ are underestimated, and the implications of its inadequacies not fully appreciated. The rest of this chapter is an attempt to elaborate some of these concerns.

Actually the difficulty encountered with h' is implicit even in cases where the pole is on a vertical plane perpendicular to the line of sight. The function $\tan \alpha = h / d$ holds strictly only for right triangles (see figure 2.3). In figures 2.1 and 2.2 the triangles illustrated for evaluating h are isosceles; they contain no right angles. Thus, $\tan \alpha = h / d$ is not directly applicable. But since the altitude of these triangles form a right angle with h, equal d in length and bisect α, $\tan \frac{1}{2} \alpha = \frac{1}{2} h / d$. For small α, this is not much different from $\tan \alpha = h / d$, and $h = \alpha \times d$ may be a reasonable approximation.

This result, however, is not general. The difficulty is only more apparent when the object is not on a plane perpendicular to the line of sight. To determine some arbitrary size h by triangulation, it is necessary to

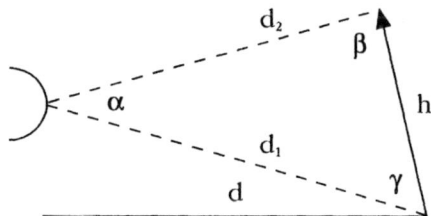

Figure 2.4   *Sources of information for a general solution to the computation of size by triangulation – line-of-sight distances* d_1 *and* d_2 *and interior angles* α, β, γ.

have information about two angles and a side or two sides and an angle. Use of tan $\alpha = h / d$ in figures 2.1, 2.2, and 2.3 depends on the fact that in addition to the value of α, we know that one of the other angles is a right angle. With two angles given, h can be computed with merely one other value, d. Without the assumption that the pole is perpendicular to the plane of the distance measured by d, there is not enough information to compute h from α and only one distance measure. To determine size by triangulation, more data are needed (see figure 2.4). In addition to α, it is necessary to know both d_1 and d_2 or, alternatively, another angle, either β or γ, and one side. The corresponding trigonometric functions for computing h are:

$$h = \sqrt{d_1^2 + d_2^2 - 2d_1d_2 \cos \alpha}$$

and

$$h = (\sin \alpha / \sin \beta) \times d_1$$

or

$$h = (\sin \alpha / \sin \gamma) \times d_2.$$

There are obviously other trigonometric functions that will work – for example, $h = d_1 \tan \alpha / (\sin \gamma + \cos \gamma \tan \alpha)$ – as well as a range of formulas that rely on comparable, but different, distance and angle measures – for example, values for certain ground distances and exterior angles. All the formulas, though, require data about more than a single distance and a single angle. For expository purposes I talk at times of choosing among these equations. In light of the issues to be considered, it would be more accurate to understand the choice as being about the kinds of data the equations employ. (Hereafter models that appeal to equations requiring two distance measures will be called "two-distance" models. Those that need information about two angles will be referred to as "two-angle" models.)

It is important to keep in mind that the distance measures to be plugged into the above equations are distances along lines of sight and that the angles β and γ are the angles formed by the intersection of lines of sight with the object. The extent to which such information is available to perceivers is a matter of some dispute. Particularly among Gibsonians, line-of-sight measures are usually rejected in favor of measures of ground distance and the slant of objects with respect to the surfaces they intersect. Suffice it to say that an appeal to line-of-sight information is compatible with the claim that features of the terrain and other surfaces play a prominent role in determining these distance and angle measures. In chapter 4 I look at models that do not rely directly on line-of-sight distances and angles, but on related ground or surface measures.

For now, let us concentrate on the line-of-sight trigonometric formulas. These are still only descriptions of the geometric properties of space, and one or another of them would have to be "psychologized" if the TAD model is to use it to specify the actual processes that underlie size perception. Of these equations, it would perhaps seem more economical and more natural for the TAD theorist to adopt a two-distance model. After all, both the two-distance and the two-angle formulas require data about the length of one of the sides of the triangle. And it can be somewhat odd to assume that we know the distance to one end of an object and not the other. This is especially so for size perception in general. As mentioned previously, for most objects (e.g., telephones, desk lamps, pens, and books) or spatial extents (e.g., desk tops, TV screens, water stains on walls and ceilings) no part or end touches the ground or is otherwise privileged. And even when one end of an object does rest on the ground, as in figure 2.4, the distance measure that would be needed for accurate computation is not this ground distance d, but d_1. Use of the two-angle line-of-sight formulas requires a different kind of supplemental information, values for β or γ, and in that sense they are further removed from the initial TAD model.

Suppose, then, that the TAD theorist adopts the first equation; the reformulated TAD model would be:

$$H = \sqrt{D_1^2 + D_2^2 - 2D_1 D_2 \cos \alpha}$$

Perceived size is a function of α and the perceived distances to the end points of the object. Size perception depends on taking distance into account, only now two distance measures must be available.[16] From a

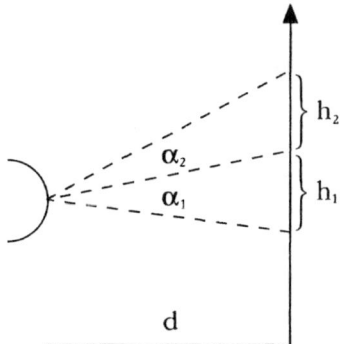

Figure 2.5   *Although* h_1 *and* h_2 *are both on the vertical plane, a single distance measure, such as the ground distance* d, *does not provide sufficient information to compute that* $h_2 > h_1$.

geometrical standpoint, all is in order again. The added bit of distance information is enough to allow for size computation. The psychological issue, however, is not one of formal geometry; rather, it is whether the TAD model, as reformulated, is a plausible account of the mechanisms of size perception. I shall return to this matter shortly. But before doing so, it seems worth pointing out that a consideration of these same geometrical facts requires rethinking the significance or adequacy of standard statements of the I.H.[17]

On one prominent formulation, the I.H. is the claim that for a given α, the perceived size is proportional to the apparent distance. The greater the perceived distance, the larger the perceived size for a specified α. As figure 2.2 demonstrates, this is not true in many cases of veridical size estimation. Except for the base point, the distances to the tilted pole are less than those to the upright pole, but the size of h' is greater than h. Similar remarks apply to the perception of afterimages and the statement of Emmert's law. Size is proportional to differences in distance (or slant), as well as to absolute distance. Once again, a relevant notion of "the (apparent) distance" is not clear. Each of the points of the tilted pole is at a different distance from the observer.

Restricting the I.H. to objects that are actually on a fronto-parallel plane will not necessarily resolve the difficulty. As figure 2.5 shows, even for objects on such a vertical plane, α_1 may equal α_2 while h_2 is bigger than h_1. So if the size difference between h_1 and h_2 is perceptible, the distance information needed cannot be merely the single ground

distance or the equivalent line-of-sight distance perpendicular to the vertical. Just as the TAD model must be reformulated if it is to apply to
more than a very limited set of examples, so must the I.H. The two
distance formula $H = \sqrt{D_1^2 + D_2^2 - 2D_1D_2 \cos \alpha}$ is one possible expression of such a generalized I.H. The two-angle formulas $H = (\sin \alpha /$
$\sin \beta) \times D_1$ and $H = (\sin \alpha / \sin \gamma) \times D_2$ are others.

Again, from a purely geometrical standpoint, nothing more needs to
be said. Any of the relevant (two-distance or two-angle) trigonometric
equations will characterize correctly the relationships among visual angle,
physical size, and distance. What need further examination are the psychological status of such an extended I.H. and the claim that the TAD
model can account for it. Perhaps the extent to which this is necessary can
be highlighted if we contrast some possible applications of the old formula, $H = \alpha \times D$, with the new TAD formulas.

Calculations made on the original TAD model seemed to involve
quite different and independent variables. There was the single perceived
distance, D, and the object's perceived size, H, that was to be determined with the aid of α and D. As I have stressed, one way to look at
the cases that force reformulation of the TAD model and the I.H. is that
they show that there is no consistently relevant notion of "the (apparent)
distance" to the object. The various points on the pole may all be at
different distances, and knowing the distance to a single point will not
enable you to evaluate size. Physical size is the extent between two points,
specifically between the object's end points. The reformulated two-
distance TAD model requires knowledge of the line-of-sight distances
to each of these. With this information, the new, stronger formula,

$H = \sqrt{D_1^2 + D_2^2 - 2D_1D_2 \cos \alpha}$, permits the size evaluation of the tilting

pole of figure 2.2 as readily as that of the erect pole. In fact, the formula
is applicable to any two points that are retinally represented. This includes not only slightly tilted poles but poles that lie on sagittal planes,
planes parallel to the ground. For that matter it includes the ground,
itself, with or without a pole (see figure 2.6).

Geometrically, in terms of triangulation, the problem of estimating h′
or the ground "distance" x to z, or determining that the distance from x
to y is the same as that from y to z, is on a par with that of evaluating
the "size" h. The amount of physical spatial separation which α represents
will be a function of the end-point distances along the lines of sight.

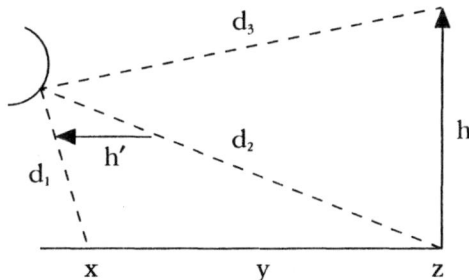

Figure 2.6   *Measures of objects parallel to the ground, like* h′, *and the ground itself,* x z, *are instances of the same general computation used to estimate the size* h.

Given this end-point data, the two-distance formula works equally well in all cases. Without such information, it is not applicable in any. But once the model is applied to tilting poles as well as those that are erect, there would seem to be no obvious principle for excluding its application to the separation between ground points, or perhaps between any two points that are retinally represented.

Using this TAD formula to compute ground distances would mean, somewhat problematically, that in seeing such distances our visual system must take perceived distance into account. Of course, there are two different distances being referred to here. The data needed as input to the computation are the apparent distances from the observer to the end points, while the output is the perceived distance along the ground. It would seem, though, that in many of the experimental studies of the TAD model and the I. H., the distance judgments solicited have been of ground distances.[18] Such judgments would not be the ones most appropriate to evaluating the present models. In fact, without further argument or reformulation of the thesis, consistency might seem to require that perceived ground distance be taken as the output of TAD calculations, rather than a datum plugged into the model. Ground distances are, after all, just certain size extents along planes that happen to lie at a certain slant from the perceiver. But why on the TAD model should spatial extents having that slant be given a different and special status than extents that lie on any other plane?

Consideration of the underlying geometry also raises some related questions about testing the TAD model and the I.H. First, in order to test a generalized TAD model it is necessary to obtain judgments for more than H and a single D. It requires values for D_1 and D_2 or, if one

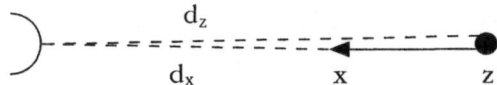

Figure 2.7   *Line-of-sight distance values required to estimate the size* x z.

of the two-angle models is adopted, values for registered β or γ. Second, although a generalized I.H. would remain merely a descriptive statement, a choice must be made from among the alternative equations that might be used to represent it. Testing an I.H. requires both specifying which psychological judgments (D_1, D_2, β, or γ) are claimed to vary with H and securing data for each of these. Third, strictly speaking, these sorts of requirements can not be avoided by limiting tests of the TAD model and the I.H. to objects appropriately located on a fronto-parallel plane. The fact that $h = \alpha \times d$ happens to hold for the actual physical object does not diminish the need for more information to test the psychological claims. For unless the perceiver can be assumed to assign values to one of these other variables, there are not enough constraints on how pairs of H and D judgments must vary in order to satisfy the psychological hypotheses. Alternatively, were the perceiver to set distance or angle values incompatible with the fact that d and h form a right angle, the predicted values of H and D should be different. It is, in a way then, misleading to represent the TAD model or the I.H. by $H = \alpha \times D$, even for those special cases in which $h = \alpha \times d$ holds.

Nothing said so far or in what follows precludes the possibility that spatial extents are really computed by taking into account line-of-sight end-point distances D_1 and D_2. Nor, though, am I claiming that it is an established fact that the visual system does make these line-of-sight distance assignments. This, I have indicated, is a controversial issue in theories of spatial perception in general. My point here is that the TAD model, as formulated, requires such information, and I wish to explore the implications of this assumption. For consideration of this issue raises some interesting questions about how we are to conceive of the relationship between estimates of distances and estimates of size.

Suppose, for example, we are looking at a pole that lies along a line of sight, a pole whose base is slightly enlarged so that only its end points x and z are retinally represented (see figure 2.7). Registered α will consist, so to speak, of two retinal points p_x and p_z. Determining the size of x, z by the TAD formula requires that the observer have available estimates of the distances d_x and d_z.[19] In other words, the observer must first assign distance significance to p_x and p_z. But in setting the distance significance of p_x, at, say, 5 feet and p_z at 12 feet, it would appear that the observer has already gone a good way toward perceiving the size of the pole.

Setups in which only the end points of objects are retinally represented are not the most usual and may be difficult to perceive accurately. Were the pole in figure 2.7 tilted slightly, however, light would be reflected from its entire length. Now although the TAD formula we are working with only requires end-point distances, the model provides no clear reason for assuming that the visual system would not also assign distance significance to the other retinal points that lie between p_x and p_z. In addition, if size perception is veridical, it would, for example, set the value of p_y, the retinal representation of the midpoint of the pole at an appropriate distance greater than p_x and less than p_z. Besides, the model needs estimates of the likes of d_y if it is to determine the lengths between x and y, y and z, and so forth. Having made all these distance assignments, though, it would again seem that in some sense the observer may already be said to see the size of the pole.

It would not be quite correct to claim that these cases show that size estimation amounts simply to being cognizant of differences in end-point distances. In the first place, when the pole is situated as in figure 2.1, $d_1 = d_2$, and the difference between them is zero. Measuring size requires assigning the registered end-points not only distance but direction. Only along a single line of sight will the difference between d_1 and d_2 simply equal size. In all other situations size will be a function of both end-point distances and their relative directional positions, as reflected in a. Second, even in cases where the pole lies approximately along a single line of sight, there is a distinction to be drawn between knowing the end-point distances themselves and knowing what the difference between them comes to. After assigning $p_x = 5$ feet and $p_z = 12$ feet, it would require an additional computation to determine explicitly that the size of the pole is 7 feet.

For our concerns, the crucial psychological issue is whether such further calculations actually occur as part of the basic processes of ordinary perception. According to the TAD model the answer should be "yes." Assigning line-of-sight distances to retinally represented points merely provides the data needed to apply the triangulation formula. Distance is taken into account only when these values are plugged into the equation and used to derive H. But how plausible is it that the visual system first sets distances along lines of sight for retinal points and then goes on to compute H values in the manner of a TAD model?

Lacking a detailed specification of the way in which an extended TAD model is to be elaborated, it is hard to say anything definitive. It would appear, however, that there are some reasons for being skeptical about this added claim. To begin with, it should be noted that once the visual system assigns to each point a distance along the direction of its line of sight, all two-point distances (sizes) are fixed.[20] The visual system will have "mapped out" its visual space. True, this mapping will not assign explicit values to separations between two-point extents, but it will constitute a particular perception of the world that, in a sense, determines what these spatial separations are. So, for example, in viewing the sky across a field, such an initial assignment of distances will already specify different amounts of spatial separation for the same value of α.[21] At this first stage too, the surface of objects will be mapped out. Each point on the visible surface of a chair, book, or basketball will have been given a distance in a direction that fixes the object's overall size. The situation may be even more conspicuous with afterimages, since in this case there is no real size to evaluate. Suppose that the illustration in figure 2.7 is taken to represent a case of projecting an afterimage of points p_x and p_z onto the world. In assigning these retinal points different distances in directions, there is a sense in which we set various of the afterimage's other spatial features too.

It might be maintained, then, that our primary visual experience of size is just a reflection of this initial mapping of space. Additional explicit calculation may take place when the observer is engaged in some special task; but such computations may not be part of the basic processing involved in space perception. Whether an initial assignment of distances "amounts to" or "is to be equated" with perceiving size will, of course, depend crucially on the definition of "perceiving size" adopted. It has been noted above that this sort of mapping could very well account for various of the phenomenal aspects of seeing size. I would stress now that it would also seem to provide much of the information needed to guide motion and reaching behaviors, activities of the kind that Berkeley argued lie at the core of our idea of "size evaluation."

By contrast, the proponent of the TAD model, who claims that a further step of deriving H values is part of basic spatial perception (i.e., that there is a distinct representation of size over and above this specification of the layout), must come to terms with another problem. In

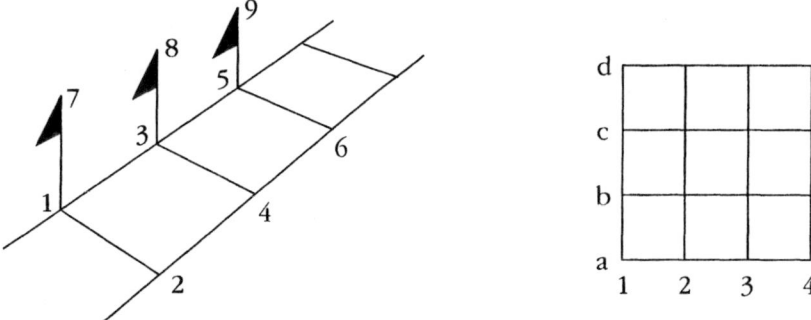

Figure 2.8   *For both standard scenes and simple figures there is a question concerning which two-point size extents are thought to be actually computed.*

order to use the reformulated two-distance TAD equation, point distances along the lines of sight are needed as data. But remember that once the information from this mapping of space is available, it is possible to apply the formula to any two points. The question, then, is which H values we are to suppose actually get computed in basic space perception.[22]

The illustrations in figure 2.8 depict the difficulty. In typical textbook discussions of size perception, we are told about applying the TAD formula to the pennants (or railroad ties) on the left. H values are said to be computed and compared for (1,7), (3,8), and (5,9) (or (1,2), (3,4) and (5,6)). These, however, are only a few of the possibilities. Theoretically, we could also derive H values for (1,5), (3,6), (2,5) or (7,6), (8,4), (7,5) or between any two adjacent or distant points in the scene. So when we describe a person as seeing size veridically, or as having constancy, which of these H values are we assuming that the person has computed? It would seem that the TAD proponent must either assume that all possible two-point sizes are computed or provide a rationale for restricting the cases.

Or consider the perception of the simple grid shown on the right of figure 2.8. When viewing this grid, do we calculate (1a,4a) along with (1a,2a), (2a,3a), and so forth? If we derive (1a,4a) and (1a,4d), do we also derive (4a,4d)? And what of the extents between all the other pairs of unlabeled points in the figure? The α and D values needed for veridical size computations will be different, as would the relevant values of registered β or γ in the case of the two-angle models. Similar questions can be raised about the TAD model's account of our perception of chairs, books, and basketballs. In perceiving an object's size with constancy, which of its spatial extents are explicitly derived by taking their apparent distances into account?

Conclusions

The aim of the second part of this chapter has been to raise and explore some problems for the TAD model. I have attempted to examine the issues from a perspective that is within the TAD tradition, rather than that, say, of a Gibsonian, who might assume from the start that the whole project is misguided. While the problems discussed do not rule out the possibility that some version of a TAD-type model could be correct, they do show, I think, that if the model is to be viable, there is need for a certain amount of reformulation and reconception of what exactly it is, how it functions, and what it claims.

A certain amount of rethinking of the statement, status, and nature of the I.H. would also appear to be in order. This would remain so even if it turned out that by appealing to a distinction between judged and registered distance, along with allowing for differences between α and perceived α, it were possible to explain away most of the evidence cited by critics of the I.H. In its standard expression, $H = \alpha \times D$, the I.H. is inapplicable. One or another of the generalized equations is needed for its representation. The apparent direct application of the formula to certain objects on the fronto-parallel plane results from the failure to make explicit that in these cases too the perceiver must be assumed to have additional information. Moreover, presenting the I.H. in its simpler standard formulation tends to obscure such facts as that: (a) veridical perception often requires that for a given α, perceived size increases as all apparent distances decrease. So, in a real sense, perceived size does not vary directly with perceived distance; (b) the fronto-parallel plane is not privileged, in that measures of α and a single distance are not sufficient to compute size in this case either; and (c) the relevant geometric relationships hold between any two points in space.

Perhaps, most bothersome of all, this formulation of the I.H. readily lends itself to the problematic conceptualization of size perception mentioned earlier: that is, treating size as linear extent on a fronto-parallel plane and distance as linear extent on a sagittal plane. Determining the length of a pencil situated on a fronto-parallel plane is thus making a size estimation, while determining the length of the same pencil pointed toward your nose is to make a distance or depth evaluation. What's more, the two problems are treated separately.[23] Adopting such an approach avoids many of the issues and difficulties that we have been considering. This "idealization" might be less problematic for models of size evaluation were it not for the fact that a preponderance of the two-dimensional surfaces we see are not perpendicular to our line of sight, and, by definition, no three-dimensional object can be located on a single such plane.

Still, in light of the body of experimental evidence that intuitively does appear to fit a claim of size–distance coupling, it might seem hard to discard an invariance hypothesis entirely. And the analysis presented here does not require that it be totally abandoned. In fact, it suggests the reverse. On the assumption that there is a stage in processing that assigns line-of-sight distances (or surrogates thereof) to retinal points, something like size–distance coupling is inevitable. For we saw that if there were such assignments, there would be a sense in which certain aspects of size perception were mapped out in the very course of setting distances. From this perspective, the supposed coupling of size and distance that the I.H. purports to describe might be better understood as a necessary consequence of any consistent mapping of distance in a direction, rather than as the going together of two separate or distinct perceptual properties, distance and size. In turn, much of the data taken to support the claim of size–distance covariance, including that associated with the moon illusion and Emmert's law, might be accounted for at this same level of processing.

It is also widely admitted that once outside the range of manipulable nearby objects, our judgments of absolute size are not very good. And our estimates of comparative size are not too accurate for objects much separated in space or on significantly different slants from one another. The lack of a mechanism for computing H values of the sort that TAD theorists propose, combined with the fact that our judgments of absolute distance are themselves not particularly veridical, may go a way to explaining these failures; but further theoretical and experimental study is called for.

How do these technical matters relate to our initial discussion of Berkeley's views about size perception? Obviously, if the problems explored in this chapter serve to challenge the TAD model, this would lend support to one major thesis of Berkeley's account of size perception. I am not maintaining, however, that Berkeley raised any of the specific, more technical issues concerning the TAD model that I have recounted. Rather,

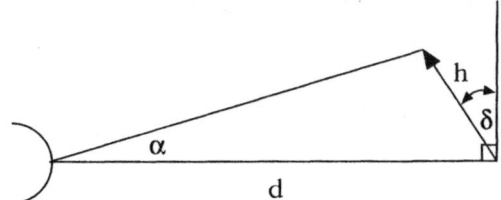

Figure 2.9 *A measure of* δ, *the slant from the vertical plane, can be used, instead of information about a second distance or another interior angle, to compute size.*

I believe that Berkeley's stress on getting clear what we mean by distance and size perception, his generally ignored arguments against the propriety of conceiving of the standardly cited cues as distance cues as opposed to size cues, and his criticism of the psychological reality of the TAD model lead to a consideration of a set of important issues that have become quite prominent, especially with recent developments in computational approaches to the study of vision. These are the questions: What gets computed and represented? And at what stage of visual processing might this be accomplished?[24]

Appendix: The Slant Model

When TAD theorists do pay heed to the problem of dealing with objects not on the fronto-parallel plane, they frequently cite the slant model as a possible solution. And it may seem that the difficulties raised about the TAD model could be sidestepped by taking such an approach. The basic idea behind the slant model is illustrated in figure 2.9. It is claimed that h can be computed from α, d, and δ according to the formula tan α = h cos δ / (d − h sin δ)[25] Further, when h is on a fronto-parallel plane, it is said that δ = 0, and this formula reduces to the standard equation tan α = h / d.

But a brief look at the geometry of the situation indicates that not much is significantly different about this approach, other than its being a two-angle rather than a two-distance model. First, like the other models, it requires line-of-sight distance data. Second, it requires supplementing values of d and α with additional information. This time it is knowledge of. Third, if δ is taken to be a measure of slant from a fronto-parallel plane, the formula remains very limited. It strictly holds only for situations where d forms a right angle with this fronto-parallel plane. So, similar questions arise as to whether and how it can be applied to cases like figure 2.4 or, for that matter, to cases where h is on a vertical plane, as in figures 2.1 and 2.5.

The slant values needed for accurate size computations are not between h and the vertical plane but between h and the plane perpendicular to the lines of sight of the relevant end points (or surrogates thereof). In most cases, the angles determined by each of these lines of sight will be different. With an appropriate adjustment in the formula, data on either of these angles will do. Once the slant equation is reformulated or understood in this way, however, variants of the questions raised earlier about the TAD model reappear. In terms of the theoretical issues explored in this chapter, the slant model need not be given separate treatment.[26]

Notes

1 Berkeley, *New Theory*, sect. 52.
2 Margaret Atherton's *Berkeley's Revolution in Vision* (Cornell University Press, Ithaca, N.Y., 1990) does discuss Berkeley's views about size in some detail. My goal in this chapter is less historical exegesis than the exploration of some problems concerning size perception that are raised by a consideration of Berkeley's ideas.
3 Lloyd Kaufman and Irvin Rock, "The Moon Illusion," *Scientific American*, 207 (1962), pp. 120–31.
4 Ptolemy is often-cited as the TAD model's first proponent, and Helmholtz as its major modern champion. Both these historical claims have been questioned.
5 The more recent, alternative, Gibsonian perspective will be discussed in chapter 4.
6 For more on this, see V. R. Carlson, "Instruction and Perceptual Constancy Judgments," in *Stability and Constancy in Perception: Mechanisms and Processes*, ed. William Epstein (Wiley, New York, 1977), pp. 217–54.
7 See Irvin Rock, *An Introduction to Perception* (Macmillan, New York, 1975), pp. 71–3, for some interesting remarks on this matter.
8 Berkeley, *New Theory*, sect. 73. For example, he points out that posture and angle of regard play a role. Angle-of-regard theories have been and continue to be among the more popular explanations of the illusion. Berkeley also allows that we ordinarily spend most of our time looking at objects situated on the ground and in the presence of other things. This too, he says, can

explain why the moon appears differently on the horizon than on the meridian.

9   For a review of some of these issues, see Tadasu Oyama, "Analysis of Causal Relations in the Perceptual Constancies," in *Stability and Constancy in Visual Perception*, ed. Epstein, pp. 183–216.

10   For an update on where things stand concerning the moon illusion in general, as well as discussion of the Kaufman and Rock solution, see Maurice Hershenson (ed.), *The Moon Illusion* (Lawrence Erlbaum, Hillsdale, N.J., 1989).

11   See, e.g., Rock, *Introduction to Perception*, pp. 34ff.

12   This is the formula standardly found in textbooks. It is derived from the trigonometric function tan $\alpha = h / d$ and the fact that for small α, tan $\alpha \approx \alpha$ in radians. But without additional assumptions, the formula is not correct. More on this later.

13   This assumption is not without problems, but I leave aside the ramifications of such complications here. See Don McCready, "On Size, Distance and Visual Angle Perception," *Perception & Psychophysics*, 37 (1985), pp. 323–34.

14   Alternatively, those theorists who believe that the empirical evidence available weighs in against the I.H. take such findings to be a strike against the TAD model.

15   If the difference between h' and h is sufficiently large, it will be perceived. Throughout this chapter, I am not assuming that size perception is always, or even mostly, veridical. I am concerned instead with the sorts of computations that might account for the facts about size evaluation in general, failures as well as successes.

16   With some adjustments, variants of my main points can be made if a two-angle model is adopted. Focusing on my two-distance model, however, provides a newer, different, and, I think, better perspective from which to examine the issues that concern me. For discussion of another two-angle model see the appendix to this chapter.

17   I leave open for now the question of whether the I.H. is correct empirically. I argue later that there is a sense in which some version of it might have to be true, even if the TAD model is false. My concerns here, however, are with problems more internal to the I.H. and the TAD model.

18   For a review of some of this literature, see W. Epstein, J. Park and A. Casey, "The Current Status of the Size–Distance Hypothesis," *Psychological Bulletin*, 58 (1961), pp. 491–514.

19   Again, nothing precludes the TAD theorist from appealing to or giving special status to ground or surface *cues* to set these distances. It does become more of a problem for the model, however, if a *measure* of ground or surface distance is needed to compute these line-of-sight distances.

20   This geometric equivalence is well known. What have not been explored by champions of the TAD model, I believe, are the implications of the fact that on a more adequately formulated model the additional line-of-sight distances, or comparable information, must be available to compute size.

21   This will be true whether line-of-sight end-point distances are used or whether some surrogate involving ground distance, height, and slant is used instead.

22   An aspect of this problem was raised earlier in questioning whether, according to the TAD model, ground distances are computed as just another case of size evaluation, or whether measures of ground distance provide data which the model needs for computing the sizes of other objects.

23   The particular example of the supposed differences in perceiving a pencil is taken from Hiroshi Ono and James Comerford, "Stereoscopic Depth Constancy," in *Stability and Constancy in Perception*, ed. Epstein, pp. 91–128, esp. pp. 91–2. As they note, however, they are falling in with a common practice, a practice found in many of the works on size perception cited in this book.

24   In my own case, Berkeley's ideas on size perception forced a consideration of these issues, independent of the newer computational studies. For more on the later work concerning these questions and in general, see David Marr, *Vision* (W. H. Freeman, San Francisco, 1982), esp. ch. 4, and H. G. Barrow and J. M. Tenenbaum, "Computational Approaches to Vision," in *Handbook of Perception and Human Performance*, vol. 2, ed. K. Boff, L. Kaufman and J. Thomas (Wiley, New York, 1986), ch. 38, esp. sect. 6. For a Gibsonian-influenced computational approach to these questions, see H. A. Sedgwick, "Environment-Centered Representation of Spatial Layout: Available Visual Information from Texture and Perspective," in *Human and Machine Vision*, ed. Jacob Beck, Barbara Hope and Azriel Rosenfeld (Academic Press, New York, 1983), pp. 425–58.

25   See W. H. Ittelson, *Visual Space Perception* (Springer, New York, 1960), for an early statement of this model.

26   Again, the central aim of chapter 2 has been to challenge certain interpretations and features of standard TAD models, not to examine alternative approaches to size evaluation, in which some of these matters may be handled more adequately.

3 Perceptual Inference

Does perception depend on inference? The question is a very old one, which does not seem to want to go away. One might reasonably have expected that advances in visual science would have resolved the issue by now; but the dispute is still very much alive.[1] Such relentless persistence of the problem, in spite of developed sophistication in our understanding of vision, suggests that something is askew. And I certainly think that something *is* askew. Indeed, I think that the problem of perceptual inference has evolved in such a way that there cannot be a single proper answer to the question. Thus it is unlikely that any simple "yes" or "no" answer could possibly prove satisfactory. Showing why this is so, however, first requires reviewing some tangled historical matters. For the current dilemma over inference is intimately tied to its checkered past. In this chapter I will talk mainly of inference. The issues that I will consider are intimately connected with the question of immediate perception discussed in chapter 1. They are also closely related to more recent debates over whether perception is direct or indirect. In fact, for many, to say that perception is immediate or direct is just to deny that it is based on inference.

Some Historical Background

In contemporary psychological literature, the introduction of inference as an explanatory concept in the theory of vision is most often traced to Hermann von Helmholtz, in particular to his *Treatise on Physiological Optics*.[2] In a section of that book entitled, "Concerning the Perceptions in General," Helmholtz proposes to talk about certain processes underlying perception as "unconscious inferences" and the results of these processes (i.e., what we perceive) as "unconscious conclusions."[3] Nevertheless, I believe that clarity and perspective can be gained by postponing an analysis of Helmholtz and looking initially at Berkeley. For Berkeley's work contains both the seeds of Helmholtz's ideas, as well as the roots of some of the later confusions.[4]

As explained in chapter 1, Berkeley claimed that all we are immediately aware of are color and light. We perceive spatial distance, magnitude, and situation derivatively, our immediate visual experiences serving as signs for these latter ideas. On Berkeley's account, the link between these two sorts of ideas is established by learning. Habit, formed by past associations, serves to connect our visual manifold and kinesthetic eye cues such as convergence and accommodation with our tangible ideas of space gained from movement and touch. It is these tangible ideas that give spatial meaning to our visual experience; the visual manifold has no spatial significance in and of itself. In turn, these tangible ideas tend to be the ideas that form the focus of our conscious attention, for they are the ideas that are most valuable in coping with the environment. Along these lines, Berkeley thought that he could provide an explanation of our ability to perceive the spatial layout, as well as an account of how we acquire such skill. He also believed that his model offered a basis for explaining various cases of non-veridical perception like the moon illusion.

Now throughout the *New Theory* and in later works Berkeley characterizes his model as one involving processes of sign interpretation – interpretation guided by past associations. In fact, Berkeley explicitly proposes that we think of these perceptual processes as akin to what goes on in understanding language. Our immediate visual experiences are, like words, mere signs of their meanings. We are not immediately aware of the ordinary spatial properties of objects, but only of a visual manifold that serves as a sign to trigger the assignment of these properties. As in the case of language, the link between such signs and what they stand for is not a necessary connection. There is, therefore, no a priori way of knowing the significance of our immediate visual experiences; we must learn what they mean. Once the connection is mastered, however, we then pay little attention to the actual sign when it is encountered. Instead, our mind leaps to the meaning or interpretation that the sign triggers.

Still, although Berkeley is quite willing to treat spatial perception as involving processes similar to linguistic sign interpretation, he is most critical of certain more "intellectualist" approaches to perception. The *New Theory*, as we saw in the two previous chapters, contains a sustained attack on the optic writers' accounts of space perception. According to Berkeley, these theorists claim that various aspects of spatial perception depend on processes of computation analogous to the intellectual-type reasoning that a geometer might go through to determine spatial layout – for example, explicit derivation of distance by triangulation, size by taking account of distance, location by projecting out along lines of sight to their point of intersection. In the *New Theory* Berkeley offers a series of arguments designed to show that explicit intellectual-like computations of the sort he believed these models required do not take place, and that the facts about spatial perception can be better explained in terms of his more associationist approach. Berkeley and the optic writers are, of course, in agreement that spatial perception is not direct, a matter of immediate experience, but requires a multistage processing of ideas. What Berkeley challenges is the specific type of processing that the geometric model invokes and the nature of the ideas involved in these supposed computations.

In the *New Theory* he uses the term "inference" somewhat indiscriminately to describe both his own processing model and that of the optic writers. In *The Theory of Vision, or Visual Language Vindicated and Explained* and in other works he allows that such usage is misleading. He argues that we should reserve the term "inference" for processes of reasoning and deduction like those found in the geometric model; for cases in which, on the basis of data about angle size, distance, and so on, we actually derive ideas according to geometric principles that we can be said to know. He proposes that we use the term "suggestion" to characterize his own model; that is, to describe mechanisms of associative triggering of one idea by another. These processes of suggestion are the work of sense and habit, not the intellect. As Berkeley says of the senses, "they make no inferences."[5] In addition, Berkeley claims that these processes of suggestion are by and large cut off from our more intellectual mental doings. We may know perfectly well that the moon is the same size on the horizon as at its zenith, yet we see it as larger on the horizon. The associative habits of size perception just run off, bringing to mind the idea of a larger horizon moon, in spite of our intellectual knowledge that the moon is constant in size.

Having briefly sketched Berkeley's views concerning inference in perception, we can now turn to Helmholtz's famous doctrines. For Helmholtz, too, spatial perception is a multistage process. Our sensory mechanism responds to light by producing certain kinds of visual sensations which have no inherent spatial significance. Sensations are to be explained physiologically, in terms of our sense organs' abilities to respond to stimuli of a given kind.[6] Helmholtz also distinguishes such sensations from our ordinary everyday visual experiences of objects in space. The ideas of spatial properties that we attribute to objects are not visual sensations, but rather ideas triggered by the sensations. The occurrence of these ideas, he argues, is not a matter of simple organic or physiological doings. It depends on learning and, hence, involves psychological processes. Helmholtz calls these second-stage experiences, those that depend on psychological processing, "perceptions." And, as Helmholtz himself says, perhaps the major strand of the argument running through his empirical and theoretical work on vision is the claim that most visual phenomena depend on learning and psychological processes and, therefore, are perceptions, not sensations.

Like Berkeley, Helmholtz uses a linguistic metaphor to elaborate his model. He says that we can think of our sensations as signs in a language, signs that by themselves have no inherent meaning. What we are immediately aware of, then, are not the real spatial properties or ideas we attribute to objects, but only signs for these ideas. "Our ideas of things *cannot* be anything but symbols, natural signs for things which we learn how to use in order to regulate our movements and actions."[7] These signs acquire their significance as a result of our commerce with the world; we must learn the meaning of our immediate visual experiences. In time, habits develop for interpreting the sensations we are physiologically given. Our ordinary perceptions are the experiential meanings that result from the interpretations we have learned to associate with our sensations.

So far, then, Helmholtz's position has much in common with Berkeley's model. Where the two might seem to diverge is over the issue of inference. Berkeley, in his more careful moments, argued that his model should not be described as an inference model; whereas Helmholtz specifically claimed that the psychological processes he proposed to account for perception should be thought of as instances of inference. Nevertheless, I think that the differences between Berkeley and Helmholtz on this score are more terminological than real.

In the chapter entitled "Concerning the Perceptions in General," where he introduces the notion of "unconscious inference," Helmholtz claims that he is doing so in order to stress the analogy between the psychological processes underlying vision and those involved in ordinary *inductive* reasoning. Helmholtz indicates that the model of inductive reasoning that he has in mind is borrowed from J. S. Mill. Consider, Helmholtz says, how it is that we are led to conclude or judge that Caius is mortal. According to Mill, the processes of reasoning can be characterized by the following syllogism:

Major premise:	All men are mortal.
Minor premise:	Caius is a man.
Conclusion:	Caius is mortal.

Psychologically the story goes something like this. First, the major premise is established by induction. It is based on the experience that men hitherto encountered have been found to be mortal. Next, we note that Caius is a man. Given these premises, the mind is moved to the idea that Caius, too, is mortal. For Helmholtz the situation with respect to visual perception is much the same. First, we learn from experience that certain kinds of sensations are signs of certain ideas about the spatial layout. This establishes the major premise. When, subsequently, we experience a sensation of the kind described in the antecedent of the major premise, it leads us to have ideas of the kind specified in the consequent. The crucial point of the analogy for Helmholtz is his claim that in both inductive reasoning and vision, the major premise is based on experience. Indeed, in a later work he suggests abandoning the terms "unconscious inference" and "unconscious conclusion" for the phrase "inductive conclusion."[8]

Helmholtz allows, however, that there are certain differences between visual inference and verbal or scientific inference. When it comes to vision, Helmholtz maintains that the major premise is usually not intellectually or consciously entertained; nor need it be explicitly formulated in language. In fact, in many cases we do not have linguistic terms capable of describing the ideas found in the major premise. The "psychological reality" of the major premise lies in the enduring habit, or disposition, of ideas of type A to trigger ideas of type B, a habit drummed into us by experience. It does not lie in any symbolic representation of "All A's are B's." But then Helmholtz claims that the same is often true of many everyday instances of inductive reasoning, as, for example, the above conclusion that Caius is mortal.

> [T]he Conviction that Caius would die might obviously have been reached directly also without formulating the general statement in our conscious-

ness. . . . Indeed, this is the more usual and original method of reasoning by induction. Conclusions of this sort are reached without conscious reflection, because in our memory the same sort of thing in cases previously observed unites and reinforces them.[9]

Experience develops in us a habit that leads us to expect that Caius will die, whether or not the major premise is ever explicitly formulated or entertained.

Helmholtz goes on to point out that there are important differences between these nonintellectualized types of inference and standard scientific inductive reasoning, in which the major premise is explicitly formulated. In the scientific cases, where the premise is explicitly represented, the premise itself can be the object of conscious reflection and can be influenced by various intellectual considerations. The linguistic representation allows for a more "critical sifting" of evidence, enabling us to take into account logical relations with other hypotheses, to trace out complicated patterns of experimental support, and to spot inconsistencies in our body of knowledge. The situation is different with perception. Such complex processes of critical evaluation are not available at the visual level. Perceptual inferences are automatic and cannot, in general, be counteracted by indirect evidence or intellectual knowledge. Being told that a particular A is not a B will not stop you from seeing the A as a B as long as the associative bonds set down by past experience are intact.[10] Helmholtz's unconscious inference, then, is not a highly intellectual matter involving explicitly formulated premises and logical reasoning. The type of processing he proposes would be better described, in Berkeley's terms, as matters of suggestion, not inference – hence my claim that the conflict between Berkeley and Helmholtz over inference is more terminological than real.

Terminological issues aside, what are important for the evolution of the debate over inference are many of the common threads that run through both Berkeley's and Helmholtz's models. Each stresses that important aspects of vision require multistage mental processing. The initial stage or input to the processing, what is immediately experienced, are sensations. Sensations are mental states; but they themselves are not brought about by psychological processing. They serve as signs for the ideas that we have of the spatial properties of the world. We do not *immediately* or *directly* perceive our ideas about the spatial layout. Our visual perception of the world goes beyond what is physiologically given to us in sensations. Furthermore, the organic processes that underlie sensations are qualitatively different from the processes that give rise to perceptions. Perceptions are dependent on and derived from prior mental states, which serve to trigger their occurrence. Finally, the link between these two mental states, sensations and perceptions, is not innate or a matter of reason; it requires learning.

For both Berkeley and Helmholtz, support for their picture of the nature of vision and visual processing came from many sources: physiology, philosophy, psychology, geometry, and dioptrics. Geometric and dioptric considerations are of particular interest, for they set the boundaries for any theory of vision. We "know," for example, from the one-point argument that distance along a line of sight is not represented retinally. We also "know" that retinal size is by itself no indication of real size, since objects of identical size but at different distances will produce different-sized visual sensations. Likewise, we "know" that our sensory experience of shape, dependent as it is on the orientation of an object to us, is itself no assurance of the object's real shape. Our immediate ideas of vision cannot be the ideas that we perceive the world to have. Additional processing would seem to be needed before the visual system can assign real-world significance to its sensations.

Now the reason why I have traced out this early history is that I think it can provide a perspective for better understanding current debates about visual inference; it can also help to explain why the problem has remained so intractable. For I believe that a large part of the story lies in the fact that the Berkeley/Helmholtz tradition has had a major impact in shaping developments in the study of vision. At the same time, their doctrines about inference (or suggestion) weave together various diverse elements of their theories. When later workers have considered the role of inference in vision, however, they have often concentrated on one or another specific aspect of the Berkeley/Helmholtz model and identified it with the notion of "inference." The result is that when people argue for or against the notion of perceptual inference, there is no one idea or claim that they can each be counted on to be talking about. Hence any overall attempt to evaluate or otherwise say something definitive about the status of *the* concept of inference will be subject to confusion.

In order to make any progress with this problem, I think it important to first separate out a number of different strands of the inference hypothesis and see what each amounts to. When this is done, it becomes apparent that assessment of these various and varied claims differ, and that we may readily accept one strand or version of a visual inference hypothesis while rejecting others. What is more, construals of what it means to say that vision depends on inference vary so widely that evidence offered by one theorist to support an inference claim may be put forward by another as a counterexample to such a claim.[11]

In what follows I will begin by distinguishing five different ideas that have come to be associated with the thesis that perception involves inference. The categories of analysis that I am proposing are not disjoint; many people and positions fall into more than one category, and on certain readings of the issues some of the categories may collapse into one another. There are also other ways of dividing up positions, as well as finer subdivisions within the categories I propose. I claim only that the scheme laid out here provides a good framework for understanding the issues and controversies surrounding the problem of perceptual inference. Each of the categories isolates an important aspect of the inference concept that has played a key role in the debates.

Sensation–Perception Distinction

This claim has two parts: first, that perceivers have both sensations and perceptions; and second, that perceptions are based on or derived from sensations. On this account, what we are immediately or initially aware of is a sensory core or phenomenal manifold that serves as a stimulus or sign for perception. Perception of objective distance, size, shape, and in some cases even properties of color and brightness result from processes that have sensations as their input. The sensory core has usually been understood to map rather directly the spatial and light properties of the retinal image: the greater the retinal area stimulated, the larger the phenomenal extent; sensory shapes are determined by the shape of the retinal image; sensed color and brightness reflect the quality of the light striking the specific retinal location. This claim, that we experience a sensory core that corresponds more or less directly to the spatial and light properties of the retinal image, came to be called the "constancy hypothesis."[12]

Understood in this way, the sensation–perception model makes two empirical claims: one about the different kinds of visual states we have the other about the processes involved in going from states of sensation to states of perception. Over the years, both of these claims have been seriously challenged. For example, one of the main thrusts of Gestalt theories of perception was to deny the constancy hypothesis; that is, to deny that we must have or experience an initial sensory state that corresponds in a one-to-one fashion to the retinal image.[13] As noted in chapter 1, the claim that our experience of a three-dimensional world is derived from a two-dimensional phenomenal manifold has been contested; and many, if not most, contemporary theorists reject the idea that when we look at a piece of coal in sunlight, we have, in addition to our perception of black, a sensation of white, reflecting the brightness of the light reaching the retinal image from the coal.

Not all challenges to the model, however, have sought to deny that we have two kinds of experiential visual states. Some theorists have been willing to accept that we have two sorts of visual states but deny that perceptions are *based on* or *derived* from sensations. One can admit that the receding railroad tracks do in a some sense "look like" they converge, are experienced visually as taking up less of the phenomenal field as they recede, yet reject the claim that the perception of the tracks as parallel is triggered by or is the result of interpreting this sensory experience. Gibson, to mention one prominent theorist, seems to take this line in his earliest book, *The Perception of the Visual World*, where he distinguishes between the visual field (something sensation-like) and the visual world (something perception-like).[14] Both states occur, but he downplays the role of the former in determining the features of the latter.

It is worth noting, too, that it is possible to accept the existence of a sensation–perception distinction for some phenomena (e.g., in the case of shape or size) and to deny that there even are two distinct experiential states when it comes to other phenomena (e.g., in the case of brightness or color). Another option would be to claim that perception does in some or all of these cases depend on an initial visual "representation" that describes or corresponds to the local features of the retinal array, while denying that this initial mapping is consciously experienced. To what extent such "non-experienced" representations of the retinal image might still be considered to be sensations or, for that matter, psychological states at all, rather than "mere" physical states, is an issue that was debated; it also plays an important role in understanding some of the other conceptions of visual inference that will be discussed.

Learning

Earlier it was indicated that for Helmholtz perhaps the main point of the analogy between the processes of vision and those underlying certain cases of nonvisual inference was the inductive nature of both. They each require a similar kind of learning. What makes a particular visual phenomenon a case of unconscious inference is that it depends upon memory traces laid down by earlier experience. If we were simply constructed physiologically so that, as a matter of our innate endowment, a given retinal stimulus resulted in our seeing things the way we do, there would be no need for the development of inductive habits. In turn, there would be no obvious reason for conceiving of such cases as analogous to ordinary inference.

On this account, the debate over inference became, and has remained for many, part and parcel of the debate between nativism and empiricism. If a visual phenomenon can be shown to be innate, this means that it is not dependent on inductively established memory traces, and hence that it should not be thought of as inference-based. On the other hand, if it can be shown that the phenomenon is shaped by experience, then there will be no explanation of the phenomenon simply in terms of innate organic structure. A full explanation will have to take into account the effects of learning, the influence of inductively established habit on our native endowment.

Although the two have often been run together, this learning criterion for inference does not necessarily line up with the sensation–perception criterion previously described. It could be, for example, that we are innately constructed so that stimulus X causes conscious experience A, which then automatically sets off conscious experience B. This would be a two-step process involving two conscious items, one of which triggers the other; yet the process does not depend on inductively established habits or memory traces. Alternatively, it would seem possible that there could be cases in which what is seen is influenced or determined by experience, but where the processing is not of the two-stage sensation–perception variety. Perhaps learning operates directly, by changing the nature of the visual experience that the stimulus X causes. Prior to learning, encounters with X cause A-type ideas. After learning, the physiological mechanisms of the system are altered so that X now immediately triggers B-type ideas without any occurrence of an A idea.

This last possibility was not really a live one for Helmholtz or for many other workers both before and after. The assumption was – and for many theorists still is – that learning cannot affect our senses per se. Learning may alter where or how we look or focus our attention; but, given the same input to a sense organ, the purely sensory output will necessarily be the same, the only exception being if the organ is fatigued or has been damaged. The outputs of *sense*, on this view, are "impenetrable" by learning as well as thought. For Helmholtz it was a methodological principle that if it could be shown that some visual phenomenon was affected by experience, the phenomenon could not be a sensation but must be a perception.[15] Conversely, part of Gibson's attack on the Helmholtzian approach has been to argue that the fact that experience affects what we see does not imply that the processing relies on memory traces in a manner that should lead to characterizing them as inferential. Our sensory systems themselves may learn to pick up or respond directly to stimuli in new ways.[16]

The situation is somewhat different with Berkeley. Although he would probably have accepted Helmholtz's methodological principle, he did not rely as heavily on learning as a criterion for inference. The inferential processes postulated by the optic writers were supposed by Berkeley to depend on necessary ideas that were not learned by experience. In contrast to his own processes of suggestion, the inferences they postulated were not inductively established.

Impoverished Stimuli

The basic idea here is that the stimulus, or the information contained in the stimulus, is not rich enough to account for the visual phenomenon being considered. Given this "poverty of stimulus" of the input with respect to the output, it follows that our visual system cannot see the spatial layout directly but, it is said, must infer it. Vision depends on inference, since it is necessary to elaborate on or enrich the otherwise inadequate input. Cases of visual inference are to be distinguished from cases in which the stimulus is not impoverished; for in these latter instances, we are able to perceive how things are without supplementing the information provided by the stimulus.

On this account, the claim that vision involves inference turns critically on whether the stimulus really is impoverished. This requires, however, that we first have a reasonably good idea of what constitutes the stimulus and what it means for a stimulus to be inadequate to, hence unable to account for, the relevant perception. But this is not a clear or unproblematic matter. On the one hand, it is trivially true that the stimulus is impoverished in the sense that, on just about any construal of the notion of a "stimulus," it is not identical with the output, the visual phenomenon. Thus it is not possible to explain the occurrence of any visual event without making some reference to the contribution of the sensing organism. The same stimulus striking a rock will produce no visual experience or judgment, no matter how rich it is in information about the environment. All stimuli are in this sense inadequate to account for the phenomena and are in this way "impoverished." On the other hand, it is equally and trivially true that a stimulus that causes a particular visual event is adequate to it in just that sense, that it is rich enough to cause the phenomenon. Given the state of the sensing organism, the stimulus is sufficient "to account" for the output of the system. On this weaker reading of what it means for the input to be adequate, there is never a poverty of stimulus problem and never any need to appeal to inference to overcome a deficit.

If an impoverished stimulus version of a visual inference claim is to be sustained in a substantive and interesting way, it would seem necessary to find a mid-ground position between these two extremes. Later in this chapter I will examine why it may be difficult, if not impossible, to settle on any one resting place as the absolute or fixed point from which to specify uniquely and evaluate the adequacy of stimuli. Suffice it to say that the sorts of cases cited in the literature as instances of impoverishment do not fall neatly into any obvious "natural kind." Nor do they provide a ready base from which to cull a single well-conceived definition of an impoverished stimulus that avoids both the two extremes. A brief look at a few cases typically cited in the literature may serve to flesh out this point.

For some theorists, examples of "phenomenal filling-in," such as one finds in experiences of apparent movement or subjective contours, are thought of as paradigm cases of stimuli inadequate to account for the phenomena.[17] The idea seems to be that since what we see, the movement or shape, is not real, it is not itself instantiated in the stimulus; that is, nothing, in the stimulus array actually moves or has the perceived shape. The stimuli, therefore, although causally sufficient, are impoverished in content with respect to the percepts to which they give rise. These cases, one might think, should be contrasted with seeing real movement and shape, where the stimuli that cause the perceptions do reflect "how things really are."

A different notion of "impoverished" may be associated with claims that phenomena of ambiguous figures, like the duck/rabbit or the Necker cube, show that inference is involved in vision. Here the situation is the reverse of the previous cases. We do not misperceive what is really there; rather, the stimulus contains information appropriate to two different percepts, and we intermittently see each one. The inadequacy of the input is thought to lie in the fact that the difference between the two percepts, say, the duck versus the rabbit, cannot be accounted for in terms of the stimulus alone, for the stimulus remains constant while the visual experience changes.[18]

Another type of ambiguity, one that has played a large role in debates about inference, has been dealt with in our discussion of the one-point argument in chapter 1. The claim here is not that the same stimulus actually produces two different percepts, but that the stimulus underdetermines the single percept that it does cause. The stimulus is ambiguous in the sense that it is compatible with a number of real-world arrangements, although the single perception that we actually have may well be veridical. It is often said, for example, that the pictorial cues to the spatial layout are ambiguous, since there are an infinite number of spatial arrangements that can project the identical retinal image. On this construal, the stimulus is impoverished in that it does not contain enough information to specify *uniquely* what the real layout is.

Whereas the first two versions of impoverishment depend on little that could be considered controversial empirical fact – people do see movement and shape where there is none, and the same retinal stimulus can give rise to two distinct visual experiences – the claim that, in general, there is not enough information in the stimulus to specify the layout has not gone unchallenged. In recent years, Gibson and his followers have been the most prominent opponents of this last claim. They have argued that traditional theories of vision have too narrowly construed the notion of a "stimulus" and the information it contains. By taking into consideration not simply retinal point values of light but certain higher-order properties of the light array – certain ratios and gradients, particularly those that vary with time and movement – the stimulus can be shown to contain much more information about the layout. They have, in fact, maintained that once the concept of "stimulus" is appropriately extended, it will turn out that there is enough information in the light array to determine uniquely what the layout is. Accordingly, the stimulus is not impoverished, and there is no need to appeal to inference to make up for the lack. We can see directly, without inference, how things are.

Attempts to discover the extent of the information available in the light array have proved to be a most fruitful line of investigation. Study has shown that the light array as a whole, especially when not limited to static instantaneous displays, does contain a vastly richer amount of data. But whether all this additional information is actually tapped by the visual system and whether there is enough information in the light array to specify the layout uniquely are more controversial matters. Although newer works on computational theories of vision tend to agree with the Gibsonian view that the stimulus is richer in information than more traditional accounts have allowed, theorists have denied that the stimulus itself contains sufficient information to determine the layout uniquely.[19]

There is another standpoint from which it is has seemed appropriate to many to deny that *any* enlarged or enriched conception of the stimulus could ever specify the environment uniquely, the difficulty being that there is always the a priori possibility that the source of the stimulus is not the normal one, but some jerry-rigged setup or hologram display designed to duplicate the light array of a real scene. Or, in the extreme, the stimulus could be caused by a Cartesian demon and not by the physical environment at all. Arguments that trade on these sorts of considerations play a prominent role in our fourth criterion of inference.

So far in this section, I have been concerned with exploring some of the ambiguities and vagaries of the idea of "stimulus impoverishment." I have spoken as if the relationship between any such impoverishment and visual inference was itself unproblematic. Establish the former, and the latter follows. This is how many workers in the field do talk. The trouble is that matters are not nearly so clear. It is not at all obvious what exactly follows, or is supposed to follow, about the nature of visual inference from the fact that the stimulus is impoverished, whatever one's favorite construal of this notion turns out to be. A route taken in some discussions of perception is simply to collapse the two notions: to maintain that vision depends on inference is just to say that the stimulus is impoverished in the specified way. Proponents of the impoverishment criterion of inference often talk as though they have something more in mind, however. The idea seems to be that if the stimulus is insufficient, inference must play a role in making up for the deficit. What this additional claim specifically amounts to is none too clear. Some writers seem to be willing to apply the term "inference" to any process or mechanism, whatever its nature, that the visual system employs to transform an inadequate stimulus into perception. On this construal, the claim that vision involves inference has little empirical content over and above the purported claim of impoverishment. It does not entail anything about the nature of our visual accomplishments and would be compatible with almost any explanation of these accomplishments.

In order for an impoverishment version of a visual inference claim to have significant empirical content, it is necessary to spell out a stronger connection between stimulus impoverishment and the role that inference is supposed to play in making up for such a deficiency. No single construal of this relationship springs readily to mind, which is not surprising. To begin with, there is no reason to assume that the three different types of impoverishment noted above, along with numerous others not discussed, would all require the same sort of account of how the visual system makes up for the various kinds of limitations of the stimulus. The duck/rabbit phenomenon, for instance, might depend on inputs from our store of memory traces of duck and rabbit experiences, whereas the phenomenon of apparent movement or subjective contours might be explained in terms of low-level interactions at the retina or a little ways in. Meanwhile, the correct account of size or shape perception may depend neither on memory traces nor entirely on early-stage neural interactions.

Each kind of impoverishment might require a different story as to how the stimulus is "enriched." Are all of them to be understood as instances in which inference plays a role in vision? If not, which theories are to be accorded this status and why? The same question arises even if we stick to a single definition of "stimulus impoverishment." Proposed accounts of apparent motion, for example, have ranged from Gestalt theories of simple electrical short-circuiting in the brain to much more cognitivist claims about how apparent motion is due to problem solving, a result of the organism's attempting to come up with the best explanation of the stimulus. The question remains, then, as to whether any and all accounts of how the visual system might cope with the "inadequacies" of the stimulus are inference theories, or whether only certain ways of enriching the stimulus are to be thought of as involving inference. If any and all, then we are back where we started. Alternatively, when impoverishment proponents attempt to strengthen the empirical force of their claims about inference, the facts about impoverishment themselves provide few constraints. Stimulus poverty is compatible with a wide range of explanations of how the visual system works. The stimulus may be deficient in the way specified; but it is another matter to spell out what it means for the gap to be closed by inferential, as opposed to non-inferential, means.

We can now see why impoverishment versions of visual inference often do not match up readily with the other construals of inference that we have considered. On most, if not all, definitions of "impoverishment," it is possible to maintain that the stimulus is impoverished without being committed to a two-stage, conscious sensation/perception model of the processing (criterion 1). Similarly, it is possible to allow that the stimulus is not rich enough to account for some particular phenomenon but be neutral on the issue of etiology. Impoverishment is compatible with the additional information or skill brought to the task requiring learning (criterion 2) or with its taking the form of an innate constraint.

If impoverishment is not sufficient to establish any one of these sorts of inference claims, it is not necessary for others we have encountered. For example, many modern-day supporters of the taking-account-of-distance model of size or the taking-account-of-illumination model of neutral color might grant that there is enough information in the stimulus as a whole to specify size and brightness uniquely. On these models, nonetheless, the processes by which the visual system is claimed to use the available information are said to be inferential in nature. Also, early visual theorists like Berkeley did not base their ideas about the need for two-stage theories of vision on claims about the ambiguity or insufficiency of information in the stimulus. Berkeley and the optic writers do not deny that there could be cues in the stimulus that could provide unique and veridical information about the layout. Their claim was that it required a two-stage model to make use of these cues. Berkeley, however, was reluctant to call all two-stage accounts "inference models," limiting his use of this term to models that postulated explicit intellectual-type processes, rather tham those that postulated only the simple triggering of one idea by another.

Mental or Psychological Operations

According to this next interpretation, to claim that vision involves inference is to claim that vision depends on distinctively *mental* or *psychological* operations and that it is not due to (or solely characterizable in terms of) purely physical or organic processes. It is assumed, on this account, that everyone more or less agrees that the end-state, the visual phenomenon or judgment, is itself a mental state. The further claim is that the processes that bring about this end state are themselves psychological. The processes of vision are thus to be distinguished from the operations involved in the functioning of our hearts, lungs, and kidneys. These latter processes may be as, or even more, complex than those underlying vision, but they do not involve mentality. Unlike vision, they are not to be characterized in terms of the manipulation of thoughts, ideas, or other mental states with intentional content.[20]

The reasons why this fourth criterion has led to a proliferation of positions on inference are not hard to find. First, there is no clear, agreed upon understanding of what makes an operation mental or psychological. Second, some theorists who adopt this criterion take it to be both necessary and sufficient for inference, while others see it as only a necessary condition. I will look at each of these issues in turn.

What does it mean for vision to involve operations that are distinctively mental? In early works on vision this notion was often cashed in either in terms of the manipulation of conscious ideas (e.g., sensations leading to perceptual states) or in terms of learning. In other words, criterion 4 tended to collapse into one of the first two criteria. In more recent times, especially with the rise of cognitive psychology and the development of computers and computer models of cognition, the push to identify the mental with consciousness or learning has largely diminished. But willingness to widen the concept of the "mental" has only led to further complications in characterizing the notion of "visual inference." For as vague as these earlier ideas may have been, nothing as circumscribed as consciousness or learning has emerged to take their place as marks of the mental.[21] What is more, if inference is equated with mental operations in general, rather than with some specific type of mental processing, then each widening of the notion of the "mental" automatically generates an additional construal of "visual inference."

Less obvious, but perhaps more significant, once the notion of the "mental" is freed from its anchor in consciousness and learning, the very sorts of intuitions that originally led many theorists to equate inference with mental operations tend to be undermined. For the important point that these theorists wished to make (or reject) was that vision involved "higher-level," thought-like states and processes, or that vision was affected by past experiences and memory traces in the very way in which thought was supposed to be influenced. Vision, that is, involved the *mind* and mind-like intentional or experiential states. The problem is that the extended characterizations of psychological processing that have grown out of work in cognitive and computer science often do not match up readily with these older conceptions of what mental participation is taken to involve.

The issue emerges clearly in Shimon Ullman's influential paper "Against

Direct Perception."[22] In this paper Ullman argues that we should consider perception direct or immediate (and hence not inferentially mediated) if the processes that transform stimuli into percepts can only be elaborated or explained in physiological terms. "If the extraction of visual information *can* be expounded in terms of psychologically meaningful processes and structures, then it can not be considered immediate."[23] Now although he gives no precise specification of what constitutes decomposition of an operation into psychological, as opposed to physical, constructs (other than that the characterization uses concepts found in psychology, not physiology), he is clear that his notion of "psychological" processing is to be distinguished from what he takes to be the more traditional views of mental operations.[24] These psychological states and processes, he says, need not be conscious or accessible to introspection or affected by experience or memory traces. Ullman seems to suggest that it is enough that the operations involve computations on states that can reasonably be construed or interpreted as symbolic or representational in nature. In fact, an example he uses throughout the article, as a paradigm case of a kind of processing that can be fruitfully decomposed and understood in psychological terms, is that of the workings of a simple calculator. For, he maintains, "certain events and components within the calculator can consistently be interpreted as having their meaning in the domain of numbers and operations on numbers."[25]

But if this is all that is required for an operation to be non-direct, not only does it match up poorly with older traditional notions of mind, but it is difficult to see how it has anything to say about what makes such operations *distinctively* mental or psychological. Few, for example, might be tempted to credit the pocket calculator with a mind or human-like intentional states merely on the grounds that its internal states may be symbolic or semantically evaluable. More important, it would appear likely that the mechanisms underlying the functioning of the heart, kidneys, and liver could also be characterized fruitfully in representational and computational terms. At some level of abstraction, a description of the workings of the kidneys may talk of representations of volume, pressure, and electrolyte concentrations, and of computations over these values. So unless the notion of what constitutes a "psychological decomposition" is more strictly delimited, the intuitions about mental versus organic operations that often underlie appeals to the fourth criterion of inference play no role.[26]

One way to salvage something of the original intent of this criterion would be to distinguish the "symbolic" doings of calculators, kidneys, and livers from those symbolic transactions that although also not conscious, introspectible, learned, or dependent on public language and social practice are, nevertheless, not purely physical. The criterion of mental or psychological operations could then be extended to include any processing that involved these "subpersonal," "subdoxastic," quasi-representational states. I do not wish to get embroiled here, however, in the voluminous debates over where and how to draw the lines between these various grades of representational or intentional involvement, lines which I doubt can be drawn in any sharp and useful manner.[27] What should be apparent is that consideration of these sorts of issues only serves to complicate further and to proliferate construals of the claim that vision involves inference.

The second broad problem with criterion 4, which was mentioned at the start of this section, is that although some theorists consider the dependence on mental operations as both necessary and sufficient for inference, others require more. Berkeley, remember, argued that not all processing of mental items should be thought of as inference. For him, inference was to be distinguished from suggestion, the simple triggering of one idea by another. Similarly, an important question remains for those other proponents of criterion 4 who do not wish to equate an inference model with any kind of mental operation whatsoever. The question is this: Assuming one's favorite construal of the notion "mental operation," what additional features must a visual process display for it to be not only a mental operation, but, specifically, a case of inference?

As best I can tell, little attention has been given to answering this question in an explicit, detailed manner, other than by recourse to versions of criteria 1 and 2.[28] The gloss usually found in the literature is that a certain visual process deserves to be thought of as inference because it is like everyday standard cases of intellectual inference. This latter claim, though, does not provide much in the way of clear and concrete guidelines for distinguishing among visual operations. Our ordinary use of the term "inference" is not restricted to cases exhibiting the Millian structure that Helmholtz championed. We distinguish deductive from inductive inference, and apply the term "inductive inference" all over the place, to drawing generalizations on the basis of instances, confirming generalizations already drawn, reaching conclusions about an individual item on the basis of other similar instances, coming up with the "best explanation" in light of the totality of our evidence, assigning probabilities to singular or general statements using any of a wide variety of sampling and statistical techniques – indeed, to any sort of reasoning that is not taken to be deductive or, in its widest use, to any activity that leads to an empirically established nonnecessary belief. The claim, then, that some visual operation is importantly like intellectual inference is vague and ambiguous.

There is, in addition, an ambiguity in the idea that a visual process resembles the process of intellectual inference, even when one particular type of intellectual inference is singled out for comparison. In saying that an operation is like intellectual inference of a given type K, we can mean something psychologically weak; namely, that the rules or principles that characterize valid verbally articulated inferences of kind K can be used at an interesting level of abstraction to specify what the visual system accomplishes or attempts to accomplish. Or we can make a psychologically stronger claim and assert that operations analogous to those that actually go on in our heads when we make inferences of type K also take place in visual processing. An example may help clarify the point. Suppose K is deductive intellectual inference. In describing such mental activity, we normally distinguish between using the rules of logic to characterize certain formal relations between premises and conclusion and characterizing the actual steps and operations that transpire in the person's brain/mind when drawing deductive conclusions. Usually, in this case, we do not assume that the steps in the formal derivation describe real-time stages in the mental derivation. The rules of logic are not employed to make a strong psychological claim about processing. In order to evaluate a claim that vision is similar to type K inference, then, it is necessary to know whether it is a weak or a strong comparison that is being made.

Again, Helmholtz is instructive here. His own claim is of the stronger sort. To say that vision involves inference is to claim that the syllogism

> All men are mortal;
> Caius is a man;
> Therefore Caius is mortal

is an account of the processing in the sense that visual processing works in ways similar to how we actually reason to the conclusion that Caius is mortal. This, of course, does not tell us very much until we are told what intellectual reasoning is itself like in such cases. Helmholtz thought that he had an answer to this in adopting the Millian model previously recounted. We often conclude things like Caius is mortal, because we have formed habits that lead from one idea to the next; thus the idea that Caius is human triggers the idea that Caius is mortal. We do not deduce such conclusions by appeal to a rule of inference like *modus ponens*; nor is it correct to think of the generalization "All men are mortal" as itself necessarily represented in ways that would make it the object of logical computations. It is by filling in the details of the comparison in this way that Helmholtz attempts to give empirical substance to his model and goes beyond simply equating inference with mental operations in general.

Criterion 4 thus offers no one simple interpretation of the claim that vision involves inference. Indeed, in many ways, it is vaguer than most of the other construals that we have canvassed. First, it awaits a principled account of what makes an operation distinctively mental or psychological. Second, if merely being a mental or psychological operation is not sufficient for a claim of inference, it becomes necessary to be more specific about what kind of inference is being held up as a model, and whether the claim is one of weak or strong psychological characterization, or something in between. Finally, if, as seems to be the case in a lot of the literature, the claim is one of strong description, a statement about actual processing, then it probably makes sense at this stage of our understanding of cognitive activity to abandon the idea that what makes it appropriate to call a visual operation inferential is that it resembles what goes on in intellectual reasoning. For if we mean by this that the visual operations are significantly like the operations underlying these intellectual functions, then evaluation of the claim will have to await our having reasonably good theories about how these intellectual feats are performed. The problem is that, at present, our understanding of the visual system is probably on a firmer footing than our understanding of the mechanisms that mediate intellectual reasoning.

Epistemological Approaches

Especially in the philosophical literature, the claim that vision involves inference typically derives from certain general considerations about the nature of empirically gained knowledge. The basic idea running through most versions of this criterion is that there is an epistemologically important difference between what we can "really" ("simply," "directly," or "immediately") see and some of the other things that we can find out about by means of vision. But it is maintained that if these latter things that we can find out about by vision cannot be seen, then they must be inferred. This distinction between what can be seen and what must be inferred is thought to have important implications concerning such matters as the grounds or foundation of empirical knowledge, the status of theoretical entities in science, and, most provocatively, the very nature of reality and our access or lack of access to it.

A major difficulty in applying this epistemological criterion of visual inference is the total lack of agreement about what can or cannot "really" be seen. (In what follows I will use "see*" for all the different construals of this supposedly special kind of seeing.) Most of the debates in the philosophical literature have been concerned with defending or criticizing one or another understanding of this notion. Setting the boundaries on what can be seen* is crucial for the epistemological criterion, since it is those things that can be found out about by vision but cannot be seen* that are said to involve inference. If X or that X can be seen*, then there is no need to infer X or that X.[29] A brief review of some of the more prominent attempts to draw a distinction between the seeable* and the unseeable* will give a feel for the wide and varied claims that have appealed to criterion 5.

In the philosophy of science the question of visual inference has usually come up in the context of discussions of the observation–theory distinction – where or whether a line can be drawn between observable objects, properties and terms versus theoretical objects, properties and terms. Defenders of an observation–theory dichotomy have argued that there are epistemologically important differences between how we find out about such things as electrons and magnetic fields and how we come to know about more ordinary objects like tables and chairs. In the case of tables and chairs, as long as the viewing conditions are appropriate, we can see* how things are simply by looking. When it comes to electrons, magnetic fields, and the like, their size or nonspatiality precludes their being seen*. We can see* their effects in a cloud chamber or in the movement of iron filings, but we can only *infer* the existence of these theoretical entities from this visual base. We can not see* them in and of themselves, because they are too small to be seen*. By contrast, most proponents of the observation–theory distinction assume that middle-sized physical objects and many of their everyday properties are things that can be seen*.

A somewhat different distinction between the seeable* and the unseeable* concerns certain properties of objects where the objects themselves may be big enough to see*. For example, a person walks into the room, and without a pause for reflection, I announce that I see that the mayor of Jersey City has arrived. But, it is argued, this statement is somewhat misleading. For although the mayor is the sort of item big enough to see*, I must infer that the person entering the room is the mayor of Jersey City. I cannot see* this, because the property of being mayor of Jersey City is not the kind of property that can possibly be seen*. It is not a *visual* property at all. We can see* a person's size, shape, color, and spatial location. We may even see* that it is a person and, more specifically, that it is a woman who has arrived. These are all visual properties of the object; but being mayor of Jersey City is not. Use of a microscope or other means of magnification cannot alter this fact. Nor is there any characteristic set of visual properties that are reliable indicators of the property. Mayors come in all sizes, shapes, and overall looks.

On both of the above accounts of see*, it is allowed that it is possible to see* a wide range of ordinary objects and many of their properties. On other accounts, the list of things that can be seen* is much more limited. That an object has the property of being circular or is a circle might seem to be a visual feature of the world. Yet, a circle viewed from many vantage points looks elliptical. There is, therefore, a lack of correspondence between our elliptical visual experience and the circular shape we find out about by vision. So, it is claimed, under these circumstances at least, we cannot see* a circle or see* that an item is circular. The visual experience does not match its object. In fact, the elliptical shape presented in experience conflicts with the true shape. We must, then, infer the presence of something circular from its misleading appearance. We can only see* those things that appear as they really are.

A somewhat different claim about the limits of what can be seen* pins its argument on the fact that sensory experience can be ambiguous (as opposed to providing a misleading portrayal of its object). The one-point argument has sometimes been used in this way to claim that distance cannot be seen*, since the visual display of distance is ambiguous. Often the claim about ambiguity is thought to be made more readily with illustrations from other sensory modalities, especially hearing. Several different events, we are told, can produce the very same sound. The rumbling of thunder and the moving of furniture in the attic sound alike. We cannot, therefore, simply hear (hear*) the thunder, because what we hear* is the exact same sound we would hear* if furniture were being moved about. Perception of either thunder or furniture involves inference from this common base that we hear*. In general, we never hear* the object itself, but only the sounds coming from it. Vision, too, is ambiguous in this way. A broken twig and a snake lying on the ground may each reflect the same pattern of light on the retina. So we cannot really see* either the twig or the snake. The only things that can ever be seen* are the color and the light that objects reflect, not the objects themselves.

Perhaps the most controversial version of the epistemological criterion does not depend directly on considerations of size, the nonvisual nature of certain properties, the non-matchingness of some visual appearances, or the fact that two unrelated items can produce the same stimulus, although all these considerations have been appealed to in support of this doctrine. Rather, the need for inference is thought to arise from the mere fact that any perceptual judgment whatsoever about the physical environment must outrun the resources of what can be seen*. We look about and determine that there is an apple on the table. At first, we may be tempted to say that we see* the apple. But, the argument goes, a moment's reflection will disabuse us of the temptation. After all, what we see* may not be a real apple at all; we could be mistaken. It may be a fake wax apple or a two-dimensional shell of the front of an apple or a hologram apple projection, or there may not be anything "out there," and a diabolical neurophysiologist or Cartesian demon may be stimulating our brain in a way that causes us to have an apple-like experience. The only thing we know for sure is that we are having a particular kind of sensory experience. This alone is what can be seen*. Anything we find out about how things are in the real world must be due to inference from this subjective sensory base.

Epistemological claims for visual inference – and there are many more than I have detailed – all rest on some distinction between what can be seen* and what we can otherwise find out about by vision. As my summary presentation of this criterion shows, however, the idea of what can be seen* has no fixed content. According to some theorists, nothing we find out about the external world can be seen*, for it is always possible that we are being deceived. Seeing* is restricted to an appreciation of our own subjective experience, or perhaps to a realm of nonphysical sense-data that interpose themselves between us and the world out there. On other accounts, all that can be seen* are color and light, and not the objects from which they are reflected. With many of the other positions, it is allowed that we can see* things in the external environment; but the set of items that are said to be seeable* varies from theorist to theorist. The options range from only the surface of objects to a highly restricted class of visual properties to the spatial layout and objects of appropriate size to molecules and atoms once sufficiently powerful instruments of magnification are available.[30]

A good deal of the debate over these competing versions of a seeable* – unseeable* dichotomy stems from the fact that they each depend on concepts and distinctions which are themselves obscure and quite controversial: items big enough to observe simply by looking versus those requiring instruments or other aids, visual versus nonvisual properties, experiences that match their objects versus those that do not correspond to how things are, items we can know for sure or incorrigibly versus those we may be mistaken about, and so on. But this is only part of the problem. Even if these distinction could all be drawn in a satisfactory manner, this would not result in a univocal notion of see*. The contrasts which the alternative readings are attempting to highlight are not the same. Thus, we might have clearer definitions of the several competing construals of see*, but no principled basis for singling out any one of them as *the* correct one. Unless a particular account of see* is settled on, however, it is not possible to give a specific content to criterion 5. Fix on one notion of see*, and X is seeable* and hence does not require inference. Pick a more restrictive reading of see*, and X cannot be seen* and hence must be inferred. More problematic still is the fact that it is most unclear what resources are available to constrain or guide the choice from among these numerous construals of see*.

By and large, both proponents and critics of these alternative notions agree on the empirical evidence. Everyone admits, for example, that detecting electrons requires the aid of instruments, that circles look different when viewed from certain angles than when viewed straight on, that there is no one set of facial and bodily features necessary to be mayor of Jersey City, that thunder can sound just like furniture being moved, and that holograms, neurophysiologists, and Cartesian demons could fool us. But they differ over what to make of this evidence, over what it tells us about which items can or cannot be seen*.

Appealing to ordinary language to resolve the issue would appear to be of little help. First, as J. L. Austin belabored, everyday use of the word "see" wanders all over the place and does not fit well with any of the standard philosophical analyses. Second, even if ordinary language allied itself more closely with one specification of see* than with any of the others, the question would remain as to whether this favored reading of see* is the one to be employed in applying criterion 5. Proponents of less standard construals of see* could insist that it is their own, albeit non-ordinary, notion that captures what is epistemologically important.

In terms of understanding the significance of criterion 5 for the theory of vision, the problem may be put somewhat differently. Granted that it may be possible to specify precisely an epistemologically relevant sense of see* and that according to that definition X cannot be seen*, does it then follow that in order to find out about X by vision, X must be inferred? That depends. On the one hand, a champion of some other construal of see* might admit that although X cannot be seen* on the restricted epistemological interpretation, nevertheless, it can be seen* on his or her own more expansive reading. Thus X need not be inferred, for it is seeable* in this less restricted sense. On the other hand, it is open to proponents of any given version of see* to stipulate that all they mean by they claim that finding out about X by vision involves inference is that X cannot be seen* in their favored sense. This latter approach vouch-safes the claim that vision involves inference but renders it devoid of real punch. For it is open to partisans of any of the other construals of see* to make the same move.

What emerges from a consideration of these difficulties in trying to settle on a single sense of see*, I think, is the degree to which the various versions of criterion 5 have little or no empirical content in and of themselves. They really have nothing to say about a theory of vision that entails anything *significant* and *disputable* about the nature of our visual skills and accomplishments.[31] I have already noted that the empirical facts cited by both proponents and opponents of epistemological inference claims are not usually issues that anyone challenges. Everyone pretty much agrees on this supposed evidence. What I now wish to stress is that accepting one or another of these versions of criterion 5 is compatible with accepting just about any empirical theory concerning the workings of our visual system, and vice versa.

Consider, for example, the epistemological thesis that all knowledge of the external world must be inferred, because the only things we can know about for sure are the qualities of our subjective phenomenal experiences. They alone can be seen*. It is hard to figure out how this argument depends on or goes to support any significant empirical claim about what is involved in vision. To admit the epistemological point, that we must "infer" that there is an apple on the table may involve accepting particu-lar views about certainty and the foundations of or the justification for knowledge. It provides no reason, however, to favor such claims as that three-dimensional vision is based on a two-dimensional sensory manifold, or that shape constancy is learned, or that a taking-account-of-distance theory of size or a taking-account-of-illumination theory of brightness is to be preferred to a relational account, or that there is not enough information in the stimulus to determine the spatial orientation of the apple, or that mental or symbolic processing is required to determine the spatial layout, or that various illusions are due to top-down influences.

Similar remarks would seem to apply to the other epistemological inference claims. And this is quite understandable. Indeed, it would be most peculiar if it were possible to derive substantive empirical theses about the nature of vision from the sorts of arguments used to support these epistemological doctrines, or if these doctrines depended critically on psychological experimentation. It is not surprising, then, to find that most proponents of criterion 5 do not provide much in the way of a detailed specification of the empirical consequences of accepting their version of visual inference. Some openly admit that their arguments are purely "philosophical," having to do with norms or logical preconditions supposedly implicit in our concept of 'knowledge." They agree that their theories have no implications for what a correct empirical theory of vision is.[32] Other writers talk as if criterion 5 is a substantive thesis about the nature of vision, mentioning that, on their account, what takes place in vision is like what goes on in ordinary cases of nonvisual inference. But the precise empirical content of their claims that finding out about X requires inference usually amount to no more than the denial that X can be seen*. They talk, however, as though the only alternative to finding out about X by their preferred notion of "see*" is to infer X. To stipulate some such particular contrastive use of the term "infer" need cause no problems. But what is does not do is enhance significantly the empirical content of criterion 5 versions of the claim that vision involves inference.

The Status of Inference

I have sketched above five broad categories of inference claims and sub-species of each of these. The list is far from complete. Study of the literature on vision would reveal a host of other inference theses that either do not fit my broad categories or do not fall within one of the finer divisions of any of them. Yet further elaboration of this classificatory scheme is not necessary to make most of the central points of this chapter, namely: (1) that the question of whether vision depends on inference is multiply ambiguous; (2) that claims that vision does involve inference are often vague and/or devoid of specific interesting empirical content; and hence (3) that no single "yes" or "no" answer to the question of visual inference is likely to prove satisfactory.

Perhaps the most obvious feature of this disarray is the enormous diversity in the types of visual phenomena that are alleged to require inference. Everyone seems to allow that there are some cases of finding out about things by vision that are inferential in nature – for example, when a detective determines that the butler did it upon viewing a pair of muddied boots in the closet, or when we decide that all emeralds are green after examining each of 100 emeralds. But disagreement sets in as soon as an attempt is made to expand the claim beyond these "paradigm" cases. The phenomena discussed and debated in the literature as candidates for inference range far and wide. They include the phenomenal qualities of experiential states (e.g., the black look of coal in sunlight or the 3D-ness of the visual manifold); any judgment whatsoever that entails a commitment to a world lying beyond our subjective experience; the appreciation of basic features of the spatial layout such as size, shape, distance, orientation, and motion; the recognition or discrimination of everyday objects; and sightings of theoretical entities.

The situation is further clouded by the tendency in much of the psychological work on perception to delimit the range of phenomena that are said to constitute the proper domain of a theory of vision. A theory of *vision*, it is held, should concern itself solely with our ability to see the basic features or structures of the environmental layout. Everything else that we come to know about through vision must require some nonvisual input. Vision may thus inform us of the color and spatial properties of an object in front of us; however, it cannot inform us of such seemingly simple facts as that the object is a chair. In order to determine that the object is a chair, we need to know the concept or label "chair". But, it is maintained, the acquisition and application of concepts or labels are tasks that lie outside the scope of what our visual system does. Even those who consider themselves staunch opponents of visual inference theses are often willing to concede that anything we find out about that does not fall strictly within the limited domain of what our visual system provides must involve inference. We do not *see* these things or states of affairs; we infer them from what is seen, from that which is exclusively the product of our visual system. What these critics deny is that the output of the visual system itself (e.g., our appreciation of color and spatial layout), depends on inference.[33]

In any case, since practically everyone admits that some of the things we find out about by means of vision do depend on inference (e.g., the butler's guilt or the color of all emeralds), the unqualified term "inferential theory of vision" is of no real use. Furthermore, given the equivocality and obscurity of the notion of "visual inference," merely restricting the domain of the thesis to a delimited set of "visual" facts or phenomena is of little help. On some prominent accounts the claim that perceiving X is inferential carries with it no commitment whatsoever regarding the actual workings of the visual system. All that is maintained is that our knowledge of X is not epistemologically basic. At the other extreme, a claim of inference may be associated with a very specific real-time account of visual processing, as for example in the taking-account-of-distance model of size perception or the take-account-of-illumination mode of brightness. For others, nothing so specific is required; vision is inferential if it depends on learning or if any kind of top-down factors have an effect on the outcome. For still others it is bottom-up processing that employs mental or symbolic representations that is the *sine qua non* for attributing inference. And for others still, the issue is resolved without examination of actual visual mechanisms, once it has been shown that the stimulus is impoverished in a given way.

Claims about visual inference, therefore, not only lack uniformity; they need not and often do not go together at all. It is perfectly possible to accept that perceiving X is inferential on one of our five criteria and reject the idea that perceiving X is inferential on any of the remaining criteria. Moreover, even within a single criterion, the same diversity and incompatibility may exist. It is possible, for example, to believe that the stimulus is impoverished, in the sense of not "matching" the real item, but to deny that there is not enough information within the stimulus to determine how things are. Or one may assume that there is enough information in the stimulus and deny that there is any sense to the notion of "matching." Similarly, for those who favor criterion 4, what constitutes mental processing, and hence inference, on one account is not considered mental processing on other understandings of this notion, and so will be denied the title "inference model."

Now I believe that these major differences among and within the criteria account for a good deal of the confusion and conflict found in debates over visual inference. The existence of these differences goes a long way to explain why a phenomenon cited by one theorist as an obvious paradigm case of inference may be so readily cited by someone else as an obvious paradigm case of non-inferential seeing. These differences also help to explain how it is that evidence and arguments presented by one theorist in support of the claim that vision involves inference may be seen by another as irrelevant or as grounds for rejecting the claim. It is not surprising, then, that the problem of visual inference has resisted resolution even though our knowledge of the workings of our visual system has expanded tremendously. What is more, given the current state of affairs, the prospects for resolving the controversy are dim.

I believe, however, that there is a relatively easy way out of the morass. It is a way that has the additional advantage of focusing attention on more substantive issues, issues that tend to be relegated to the background once the hoary "problem of inference" begins to loom large. My suggestion is simply to give up on the question of visual inference and refrain from using the concept in our theories of vision. For not only is the claim that perception depends on inference multiply ambiguous, vague, and often reliant on dubious concepts and distinctions, but there is at present no real payoff in settling the question. The real payoff lies elsewhere, in some of the more detailed and specific claims that I have sketched in the course of presenting my classificatory scheme. This is where the action is, or at least, where is should be. In putting forth this recommendation, I am not suggesting that the mere abandonment of the term "inference" will solve all or any significant problems in the theory of vision. Rather, I am arguing that undue concern over inference has tended to obscure some real empirical problems of the theory of vision and, perhaps more perniciously, has often made it seem as though there were real substantive issues at stake where there are none.

An example may flesh out my point. I am looking at a coffee cup from an angle that projects the top of the cup as an ellipse on my retina. From this angle the cup looks phenomenally distinct from how it would appear were it tilted so that it projected a circular image on my retina. Nevertheless, I both intellectually judge or assert that there is a round cup on the table, and I spontaneously behave in ways appropriate to this being how things are. Is my perception, or some aspect of my perception of the cup, a case of visual inference? By now it should be apparent that with all the unclarity in the question, there is no telling how to respond. Suppose one persists, however, in seeking an answer. What are the options?

In order to apply the sensation/perception criterion, it would first be necessary to spell out reasonably precisely which states are to count as sensations versus perceptions and what sort of transition between them one has in mind. It would then be necessary to show that a correct description of my perception of the cup actually involved stages and dependencies of the kind so specified. This done, it would seem that nothing is added in being told that this shows that inference is involved. Nor would anything be gained by disputing the claim that the correctness of the model showed that vision was inferential.

Consider next the criterion of learning. To apply this criterion, it is first necessary to be quite clear about which aspect of the situation it is being claimed that learning plays a role in. If it is the intellectual or verbal judgment that the item is a round cup, then, unless one believes that the concepts invoked are innate, learning would seem to be required. If, instead, it is a less intellectualized appreciation of shape constancy that is at stake, then one is faced with a problem that appears to have more empirical bite. Just what the empirical bite is, however, will depend on how one distinguishes learning from triggering, maturation, and so forth. This itself is no easy matter. Finally, one would face the quite delicate experimental problem of determining if that particular aspect of shape perception depended on the form of learning specified. Once this empirical issue were settled, though, how profitable could it be to continue debating whether the influence of that sort of learning means or does not mean that vision is inferential?

Similar remarks apply to the poverty of stimulus criterion. Use of this criterion cannot get off the ground until we are provided with a fairly precise sense of what "stimulus impoverishment" amounts to. Depending on how this notion is construed, the claim that the stimulus is impoverished will range from an a priori truth, that the stimulus taken as a physical energy is not identical with either the subjective experience or the perceptual judgment, to a claim about what a detailed analysis of the optical array will show about possible sources of information regarding the cup-like shape of the object. Having adopted a single definition of "stimulus impoverishment" and having determined that the stimulus is or is not so impoverished, there would seem little point in arguing about whether impoverishment of that sort really entails that vision involves inference.

According to criterion 4, perception of the cup requires inference if it depends on mental or psychological processing. In this case, in order to apply the criterion, it is necessary to spell out exactly what constitutes mental or psychological processing and then go about determining if processing of that kind actually takes place. As things now stand, however, the types of processing models that have been said to fall under this rubric have ranged from just about any account of underlying mechanisms to only cases in which conscious items or ponderings are brought into play. I, at present, do not see any obvious grounds for deciding among all the options and thus, on this score, see no exclusive authorative basis for labeling some processes "inferential" and others "non-inferential." Nor do I see what is at stake for a theory of vision in reaching such a decision. For once we discover what the underlying mechanisms are, we will know all that it is important to know for an understanding of visual processing. Fervent declarations that such processing shows that vision really does involve inference will provide no more insight into the nature of our visual accomplishments than fervent denials that inference is so implicated.

Finally, although proponents of criterion 5 often favor one or another empirical theory of vision, I have argued that the epistemological issues that underlie their claims are largely independent of these theories. Empirical inquiry is not going to determine the "correct" definition of see*, and conversely, allowing for a difference between the seeable* and the unseeable* will not entail anything significant about which empirical theory or theories of vision is or are correct.

The claim that vision involves inference gets its life from the idea that what goes on in vision is in some way analogous to what goes on in intellectual or conscious inferential reasoning. Needless to say, playing up analogies is often very helpful in scientific theorizing. I have attempted to show, however, why I believe that in this particular case the strategy has outlived its usefulness. Neither championing the cause of inference nor defending vision from the inference metaphor is likely to have a serious payoff. In addition, I think that the debates and controversies over inference have tended to misfocus attention on vague slogany statements of doctrine instead of on the details and empirical content of the competing accounts. This is doubly unfortunate, since in many cases what is bothering people is not the particulars of the empirical content of the proffered explanation, but the aura that has come to surround the claim that vision is or is not inferential. For the claim carries with it, in the minds of both adherents and critics, a host of controversial and obscure theses, metaphysical commitments, and assumptions associated with the numerous positions outlined in my classificatory scheme.

The Temptation of Inference

I have offered a rather simple, if not simplistic, solution to a problem that has vexed the theory of vision for several hundred years. My solution is both to abandon the problem and to stop worrying about the meta-theoretical concepts, distinctions, and dichotomies needed to sustain and breathe life into the issue. My suggestion, then, is to dissolve the problem of visual inference, rather than attempt to resolve it. Unfortunately, as with many an unworthy human pursuit, merely being *told* to give up on a problem will not make it go away. Exorcism often requires uncovering the underlying causes that make the issue, even if illusory, seem so pressing. My review of the historical background and the shifts in the interpretation of the notion of visual inference was intended to reveal some of the factors that have contributed to the prominence of the question. But there is another potent assumption that provides much of the impetus for pursuing the question of inference and trying to come up with a definitive answer. It is, moreover, an assumption that can be found embedded in versions of each of the major criteria canvassed. It is the conviction that something in vision must be *given*, what the world presents or foists upon our senses.

The given constitutes the data or starting point, and all else requires that we go beyond the given. This differences, between something given as data and those ideas achieved by going beyond, is thought important, since it provides a basis for distinguishing between what the mindless world offers as evidence and what we sentient intentional organisms add in the course of interpreting this evidence. In other words, it is a distinction between the contribution that *nature* makes to our visually gained knowledge and the contribution that *we* make. In turn, this distinction is thought to have significant implications for an array of "deep" philosophical and psychological doctrines about mind and reality and the ability of the former to grasp or be in ("direct") contact with the latter.

Now it is not my intention to take sides here on any of these perplexing epistemological and meta-theoretical issues. I believe instead that there is good reason to stop most of these debates a step sooner, before they ever get off the ground. For one of the main things that emerges from the account of the status of inference is that the very distinction between the given, or data, and that which lies beyond cannot be drawn in the hard-and-fast way necessary to support these more global doctrines.

From the standpoint of an empirical theory of vision, there would seem to be no unique basis for singling out as *given* any one aspect or stage in the chain of events that culminates in perception.[34]

This lack of a firm ground for fixing the domain of the given is mirrored in the range of inference claims examined in our classificatory scheme. A way to look at the differences among and within these criteria is to see that they each depend on a particular view about what counts as given. On traditional versions of the sensation–perception approach, for example, the given is the initial conscious sensory state. Nature (physics and physiology) determines which sensations we have and what they are like. This first stage may itself depend on all sorts of complex states and processing, but, according to proponents of this criterion, nothing counts as data until it is registered consciously. It is in going beyond these conscious sensations that we make our contribution. ’

On the learning criterion, what is given is how we see the world independent of the effects of learning. Any visual phenomenon that shows the influence of learning is, therefore, the result of our going beyond the given. Such phenomena are not the sole responsibility of the world (nature) but depend on our learning histories (nurture). What is given according to the third criterion is the stimulus or the information contained in the stimulus. This is the world's input. To the extent that this input is impoverished with respect to the ultimate perceptual experience or judgment, we must go beyond the given. Our contribution lies in closing the gap between input and output. Within this criterion alternative interpretations of stimulus impoverishment will result in different understandings of the nature and extent of the gap. Still, the idea of an impoverished given is to be found in each of these accounts.

A somewhat different given–taken distinction underpins versions of the fourth criterion of inference. According to this criterion visual states and processes can be divided into two kinds, the mental (or psychological) and the non-mental (or physiological). On certain recent construals of this criterion, mental processes are understood to involve the manipulation of symbols or other semantically evaluable items that need not be conscious or learned. The given, on this account, are the first items triggered by retinal stimulation that employ explicit mental representations. It is in thus crossing the border of the purely physical that these items can serve as "data."

Perhaps the most direct appeal to a given–going beyond dichotomy is found in the case of the epistemological criterion. On this account, the given is what can be seen*; this is the foundation or bedrock for empirical knowledge. It is how the world impinges on and provides evidence to a knowing subject. We go beyond the given whenever our knowledge extends beyond what we see*. Each construal of see* determines a different set of items that are accorded the status of being given. In terms of a theory of knowledge, what has traditionally been supposed to be important about the given is that it possesses some unique epistemological properties that give it a special place in accounts of the justification of beliefs. The given is the certain or indubitable or incorrigible base for the rest of what we come to know. Nowadays, the idea that there is a set of perceptual items that is epistemologically privileged in this way has lost most of its appeal. What has not lost its appeal, however, is the conviction that perception must start somewhere, that it must ultimately be based on some data or evidence that is *given* to us, even if our knowledge of this data is not assumed to be mistake-proof or error-free.

Although each of our criteria differs in its definition of "visual inference," each account appeals to a distinction between some items that are data and other items that are inferred from these data. Each distinguishes between something given and something we achieve by going beyond this starting point. The various accounts differ only over where to draw the line between the world's contribution and our own. They each assume, however, that there is a unique line to be drawn. Which approach is it, then, that picks out the "correct" given, the "real" data or starting point for vision?

No principled, unequivocal way to make this decision is forthcoming. For the contrast between what is given and what lies beyond is, in the end, a contrast between what we contribute to vision and what comes about independent of our supplementation. But the notion of what "*we* supplement," like the notion of the "given," is not fixed and varies with theoretical projects and interests. In fact, an alternative way of looking at the relationship between competing concepts of the given and our classificatory scheme is to see each of the numerous criteria as focusing on a particular understanding of what constitutes supplementation. According to criterion 1, what counts as supplementation (our contribution) is any idea brought to mind by a previous consciously represented idea. The given, or world's contribution, then consists in the initial ideas not so triggered (i.e., sensations). The kind of supplementation central to criterion 2 is different. Supplementation here is identified with learning. If our contribution is understood as the supplementation to vision made by learning, then those aspects of perception that do not depend on learning are given.

In the case of criterion 3, supplementation is understood as providing whatever is needed to make up for deficits in the stimulus. What counts as supplementation, therefore, is a function of the construal of stimulus impoverishment that is adopted. At one extreme, the stimulus is not impoverished at all, since it is sufficient to cause whatever perception we have, and so there is no need for supplementation by us. What is given, at least in the case of veridical perception, is the world as we take it to be, or the layout or affordances that the environment provides. At the other extreme, all perception is said to require supplementation, since the physical energies that strike our retina and stimulate us to see are not identical with the perceptual experiences and judgments they cause. On this account, what are given are the values of those physical stimulus energies to which our retinas are capable of responding.

The fourth criterion likewise provides a variety of givens. Supplementation here is identified with the manipulation of mental or psychological items. This is our contribution. In turn, the given is the initial, perhaps symbolically represented input into the visual system. Finally, we find the same relativity of the given to supplementation in the epistemological criterion. For some, vision involves supplementation whenever we reach any conclusions about the external world. Therefore, what is given, unsupplemented, is only our subjective experience. For others, supplementation is more restricted, and our contribution is less. The given may be light and color or the surface of an object or the object itself as long as it is of sufficient size.

The ideas of a given and supplementation are thus intertwined. Understand supplementation one way, and our contribution is X and the data are Y. Focus on a different type of supplementation, and relative to this construal our contribution is W, and the data Z. The question of what is given in vision per se has no answer, for the data are always specified relative to a kind of supplementation. The problem with the notion of "the given" is not that we cannot make sense of specific notions of input or data to a system. It is with the term "the" and its implications of uniqueness. We could zero in on one concept of the given if we could single out one kind of supplementation as the hallmark of our contribution. Alternatively, if we had an independently specifiable notion of the given, then our contribution might be identified with whatever it takes to supplement this. But neither of these options seems to be a live possibility.

The problem of inference has loomed large, I have argued, in part because of the prominence of the conviction that there is some hard-and-fast distinction to be drawn between the world's contribution and our own, between the given and going beyond. Even the revolutionary Gibson felt that he could turn his back on inference only by claiming that all is given in vision as long as we can resonate to or are attuned to picking it up. If all is given, there is no need for supplementation or "enrichment." There is no gap for us to bridge. "The perceiver does not *contribute* anything to the act of perception."[35] Critics of Gibson find this too much to swallow. Vision must start somewhere; there must be a difference between the input to vision and the finished product. So there must be a place for supplementation, a place where we make a contribution. But the "given" and "our contribution" are not independent ideas. By emphasizing different types of supplementation, you get different givens and different gaps between the given and what lies beyond.

Once this relativity of the given–going beyond dichotomy is admitted, it becomes easier to adopt the insouciant attitude to the problem of visual inference urged in the previous section. For in all its forms the notion of inference depends on there being a gap between the premises and the conclusion, between the data given and the hypothesis arrived at. The problem is that there is no single, exclusively right way to draw this line. On the one hand, it is possible to maintain that all is given and hence that there is no need for inferential supplementation. On the other, it is possible to maintain that all perception requires inferential supplementation because visual experience and judgments are never themselves "simply" given. But I believe that there is no pressing need to defend either of these extremes or to fix on any specific place in between. For there are no firm grounds for settling on a unique construal of the given–supplementation divide, and consequently there is no one way to distinguish between *the* data and *the* inferred.

Conclusion

I earlier suggested abandoning the question of whether vision involved inference on the grounds of multiple ambiguity, vagueness, and lack of empirical content. I have now argued that there is something misguided in a key presupposition needed to get the whole issue started. Any concept of inference requires, at minimum, a distinction between premises and conclusion, between data and what is derived from data. There must be a gap for inference to bridge. May claim in the last section was that where one draws the boundaries between input and output and whether there is a gap between them are from the standpoint of a science of vision largely strategic and, in that sense, optional decisions. There is no decisive non-relativized way to settle on what is given and what goes beyond, and thus no conclusive answer to the question of visual inference. Pulling away from the debate over inference, however, will not solve or dissolve the serious, empirically significant issues in the theory of vision; but it will keep us from wasting time on a lot of bogus controversies. For if it becomes less pressing to decide whether vision is or is not inferential, it may also come to be seen as less important to settle on fixed boundaries between *the* sensed and *the* perceived, *the* innate and *the* acquired, *the* intrinsic stimulus information and *the* extrinsic sources of information, *the* mental and *the* non-psychological, *the* seen* and *the* unseen*. And once these dichotomies lose their attraction, much of the air should be knocked out of debates over whether vision is direct or non-direct or whether a realist or anti-realist account of vision is correct.

Notes

1   It would be impossible to list even a small portion of the vast philosophical and psychological literature, both old and new, on this topic. A citation count might well reveal that in recent years, debate over a paper by Jerry Fodor and Zenon Pylyshyn, "How Direct is Perception? Some Reflections on Gibson's 'Ecological Approach,'" *Cognition*, 9 (1981), pp. 139–96, has garnered the most attention. I consider this paper further in chapter 4, which is devoted primarily to an examination of the ideas of James J. Gibson.

My concerns in this chapter, however, are much more general and in the end deflationary. Here I question the significance of claims about inference, as well as the significance of the intuitions that underlie these claims. In light of this it does not seem appropriate or feasible to discuss in detail particular theorists' positions. Hence there is no separate discussion of, say, the rich body of work of Fred Dretske or Irvin Rock on the topic; but see Fred Dretske, *Seeing and Knowing* (University of Chicago Press, Chicago, 1969); *idem, Knowledge and the Flow of Information* (MIT Press, Cambridge, Mass., 1981); and Irvin Rock, *The Logic of Perception* (MIT Press, Cambridge, Mass., 1983). The bearing of this chapter on some of their views and those of Fodor and Pylyshyn should, nonetheless, be apparent.

2   Hermann von Helmholtz, *Treaties on Physiological Optics*, ed. James Southall, 3 vols (Dover, New York, 1950).

3   Ibid., vol. 3, pp. 1–37.

4   In limiting my discussion to Berkeley and Helmholtz, I do not mean to suggest that the central themes about inference are found only in their works or are due to them alone. As major players in the history of visual theory, however, their views did significantly influence the development of ideas on this matter.

5   Berkeley, *Three Dialogues between Hylas and Philonous*, Dialogue I, pp. 174–5.

6   More accurately, Helmholtz's position is that the nature of our sensations is determined not by the qualities of the stimulus per se, but by the kind of sense organ stimulated. For example, anything that triggers the optic nerve to fire will result in a visual experience. A blow to the head that stimulates the optic nerve will cause us to have visual experience, just as light striking the retina does. This view of sensory experience was underscored for Helmholtz and others by the work of Johannes Müller and his theory of the specific energies of the senses.

7   Helmholtz "Concerning the Perceptions in General," in *Physiological Optics*, vol. 3, p. 19.

8   See Helmholtz, "The Origin of the Correct Interpretation of our Sensory Impressions," in *Helmholtz on Perception: Its Physiology and Development*, ed. Richard Warren and Roslyn Warren (Wiley, New York, 1968), pp. 255ff.

9   Helmholtz, "Concerning the Perceptions in General," p. 25.

10 These days this idea might be expressed by claiming that vision is modular or informationally encapsulated or involves subdoxastic states.

11 To mention but a single representative example, Gilbert Harman in his book *Thought* (Princeton University Press, Princeton N.J., 1973), p. 175, cites the fact that texture gradients influence distance perception as empirical evidence in favor of his claim for perceptual inference. By contrast, for the psychologist James J. Gibson, the discovery of this role of texture gradients was one of his main early reasons for rejecting an inference approach. See Stephen Stich, "Beliefs and Subdoxastic States," *Philosophy of Science*, 45 (1978), pp. 499–518, for still another approach.

12 It is not necessary, however, to think of this experiential core as an object, such as sense-data theorists might propose. Further, the constancy hypothesis was so understood as to be compatible with Müller's specific energies claim, that the quality of the visual experience is determined by the nature of the sense organ, not the stimulus. It was also taken to be in line with the view that there is no identity or necessary likeness between the properties of the stimulus and those of the phenomenon it triggers.

13 See K. Koffka, *Principles of Gestalt Psychology* (Harcourt, Brace and World, New York, 1935).

14   James J. Gibson, *The Perception of the Visual World* (Houghton Mifflin, Boston, 1950). Variations of this theme can be found in his later works as well.

15   See Helmholtz, *Physiological Optics*, vol. 3, pp. 12ff.

16   For a discussion of this issue, see J. J. Gibson and E. J. Gibson, "Perceptual Learning: Differentiation or Enrichment?," *Psychological Review*, 62 (1955), pp. 32–41.

17   An example of apparent movement is where we experience movement between flashing stationary lights. Subjective contours are cases in which we experience a shape looming out of the background, although nothing in the stimulus outlines the perceived contour. See E. Sigman and I. Rock, "Stroboscopic Movement Based on Perceptual Intelligence," *Perception*, 3 (1974), pp. 9–28, and Irvin Rock, "Inference in Perception," in *PSA 82*, vol. 2, ed. P. Asquith and T. Wickles (Philosophy of Science Association, East Lansing, Mich., 1983), pp. 525–40.

18   See, e.g., R. L. Gregory, "Perceptions as Hypotheses," in *Philosophy of Psychology*, ed. S. C. Brown (Macmillan, London, 1974), pp. 195–210. See also for related issues Julian Hochberg, "Higher-Order Stimuli and Inter-response Coupling in the Perception of the Visual World," in *Perception: Essays in Honor of James J. Gibson*, ed. R. B. Macleod and H. L. Pick (Cornell University Press, Ithaca, N.Y., 1974), pp. 17–39, and "On Cognition in Perception: Perceptual Coupling and Unconscious Inference," *Cognition*, 10 (1981), pp. 127–34.

19   See, e.g., David Marr, *Vision* (W. H. Freeman, San Francisco, 1982), or Shimon Ullman, *The Interpretation of Visual Motion* (MIT Press, Cambridge, Mass., 1979).

20   Although I tend to use the terms "mental" and "psychological" interchangeably, the concepts are not equivalent for all theorists. The ramifications of making such a distinction, as well as distinguishing them both from intentional states, are discussed later on in this chapter and in chapter 4.

21   Various of my subsequent points about the lack of fixity of the notion of "visual inference" are related to the current discussion regarding consciousness and "the" time and place of conscious events (see Daniel Dennett, *Consciousness Explained* (Little, Brown Boston, 1991)). Tracing these connections would take us far afield from the present study.

22   Shimon Ullman, "Against Direct Perception," *Behavioral and Brain sciences*, 3 (1980), pp. 373–415.

23   Ibid., p. 374.

24   Ibid.; see around pp. 375 and 380.

25   Ibid., p. 380.

26   Ullman's suggestion (ibid., p. 374) that the distinction between what can and cannot be decomposed may be "relative to the system under investigation" and "expresses a point of view" about "one's domain of interest"

would seem to fit with views I develop at the end of this chapter concerning the optionality of the inference/non-inference dichotomy.

27   See article my "*The* Problems of Representation," *Social Research*, 51 (1984), pp. 1047–64, and remarks toward the end of this chapter and the next. The issue has become even more otiose with the development of connectionist models of cognition and debates over whether these models appeal to "real" representations. See Paul Smolensky, "On the Proper Treatment of Connectionism," *Behavioral and Brain Sciences*, 11 (1988), pp. 1–74, and the subsequent criticisms, countermoves, and counter-countermoves.

28   An exception would be Irvin Rock's consideration of aspects of this issue in *Logic of Perception*.

29   To simplify the presentation, from here on I drop "or that X" and use X for either or both as appropriate.

30   Some have even claimed that unmagnified molecules and atoms can be seen* (or seen, since at this extreme the epistemological force of the distinction breaks down). Norwood R. Hanson's *Patterns of Discovery* (Cambridge University Press, Cambridge, 1965), ch. 1, contains an influential statement of this view.

31   I emphasize the terms "significant" and "disputable" here, for I am not saying that they have no empirical implications. My point is that the empirical implications that they may have tend to be trivial or not a matter in serious question.

32   For an account of aspects of this matter, see Roderick Firth, "Sense Experience," in *Handbook of Perception*, vol. 1, ed. Edward Carterette and Morton Friedman (Academic Press, New York, 1974), pp. 3–18.

33   One wants to distinguish this claim that any phenomenon depending on or exhibiting the influence of intellectual or top-down mental input is a matter of inference from versions of criterion 4 that pin the doctrine on bottom-up processes that are mental or employ representations.

34   I am not claiming that there are no useful ways to divide up or classify types or stages of visual processing. The problem comes in attempting to assign one of them the special status needed to underwrite supposedly important and controversial theses about vision and inference. In chapter 4 I say some more on this topic, especially as it arises in the context of the debate between the Gibsonians and Fodor and Pylyshyn.

35   James J. Gibson *Reasons for Realism: Selected Essays of James J. Gibson*, ed. Edward Reed and Rebecca Jones (Lawrence Erlbaum, Hillsdale, N.J., 1982), p. 89.

4 A Gibsonian Alternative?

Throughout these essays I have made frequent, if sketchy, references to the important work of James J. Gibson. Gibson specifically names Berkeley as an originator and major proponent of the long-dominant paradigm of visual theory which he, Gibson, wishes to overturn. This chapter is intended neither as a defense of Berkeley nor as a criticism of Gibson. It is rather an attempt to clarify several core issues that supposedly distinguish their approaches to the study of vision. It is also an attempt to offer a perspective from which it may be possible to defuse some of the current heated debates over Gibsonian doctrines. Of course, the success of this enterprise depends in part on getting Berkeley's and Gibson's views about vision correct, a task I find more daunting in the case of Gibson than of Berkeley. Gibson's positions developed and changed during his career. His views are not always clear, and they do not seem to be entirely consistent. Proponents, as well as critics, interpret Gibson's major concepts and claims in conflicting ways.[1]

This chapter does not attempt to present a complete account of Gibson's rich ideas and evolving theories. It begins by painting with broad brush strokes a comparative picture of Berkeley and Gibson concerning the specific problems of distance and size. Doing this, I hope, will bring together themes of chapters 1–2, while shedding light on Gibson's contributions to the study of these topics.[2] The chapter ends with a consideration of that most discussed and contested of Gibsonian theses, the claim that perception is direct. This doctrine has often been taken to be what is especially distinctive, significant, and controversial in Gibson's theory of vision. My analysis of this issue draws heavily on arguments in chapter 3 concerning the status of perceptual inference.

Some Important Agreements

In his book *Principles of Gestalt Psychology*, Kurt Koffka proclaims that *the* central question in the theory of perception is "Why do things look as they do?."[3] Interestingly, both Berkeley and Gibson have reservations about putting matters in just this way. They do not ignore the question, but they call attention to certain ambiguities in its interpretation. For Berkeley and Gibson, the main function of vision is to provide knowledge of the environment. It is not to provide experiences having distinct phenomenal visual qualities. This is a central aspect of Berkeley's claim that visual phenomena serve as signs for the tangible. Berkeley plays down the significance of our fluctuating subjective visual experiences. The primary use of vision is to tell us about "reality," which in the *New Theory* is characterized in terms of the properties of the permanent tangible world. Vision serves to guide behavior. It informs us of those aspects of the environment that play a role in the pragmatic organization of our activities.

In his later, more explicitly idealistic and immaterialistic works, Berkeley seems to identify the real with sets of ideas or possible ideas from any of the senses, not only touch. If Berkeley is understood as adopting this sort of phenomenalistic ontology, construing physical objects as sums of experiences from all sense realms, then in vision we are as much "in touch" with these "physical" objects as we are when we experience them tangibly.[4] Even in terms of Berkeley's earlier *New Theory*, though, experienced tangible ideas can alert us to visual ideas that may follow, and in that sense the tangible can serve as a sign of the visible.

Still, tangible ideas take precedence over the visible realm for Berkeley. According to him, our tangible ideas provide a stability to our evaluations of the spatial layout. Our tangible ideas of a specific size, for example, do not vary in the way that our immediate visual ideas of an object of that tangible size fluctuate with the distance and orientation of the perceiver. Furthermore, tangible ideas remain pragmatically most important, in that they are the ones that affect our well-being and so must guide behavior.

Gibson too downgrades the significance of our fluctuating, "subjective" visual experiences. In his ground-breaking first book, *The Perception of the Visual World*, Gibson distinguishes between our experience of the visual field and our experience of the visual world.[5] He says that his idea of a visual field corresponds, more or less, to the older notion of "sensation." The visual field is the experience we have when we adopt an analytic attitude and focus on the qualitative phenomenal aspects of how things appear. This analytic attitude is thought to be one that a painter might adopt when trying to figure out the best way to render a scene so that the picture looks like what it represents. The qualities of the visual field, on Gibson's account, are largely in accord with the absolute properties of the retinal image, as the traditional constancy hypothesis supposed. Thus, in our visual field experience the parallel lines of railroad tracks going off into the distance converge, in keeping with the convergence of their images on the retina.

By contrast, the notion of the "visual world" is more allied with the idea of "perception," in that it is part of what we find out about the objective world by means of vision. In our experience of the visual world, the railroad tracks are parallel; they do not converge as their retinal images converge. It is the visual world that is the focus of attention in normal seeing. Most significantly, though, Gibson denies that the visual field – visual world distinction is a processing distinction. In particular, he denies that our experience of the visual world depends on intermediate steps or stages of mental activity. Both the visual field and the visual world are to be explained as sensations usually were, as noncognitive reactions of the visual system to properties of the stimulus. Accordingly, Gibson eschews characterizing our appreciation of the visual world in terms of belief, judgment, or hypothesis, terms that suggest more intellectual or mental happenings. We sense, see, or perceive the visual world; we do not infer, judge, or construct it by ratiocination.

It is largely for this reason that Gibson is willing to agree that the proper goal of a theory of vision is to answer Koffka's question. Gibson remains at odds with the Gestaltists in his account of the visual field – visual world distinction and in much of his account of the workings of the visual system. Gibson believes, however, that he joins the Gestaltists in rejecting the idea that the output of the visual system is intellectual or propositional in nature. What a theory of vision must explain is how the visual system yields sensory perceptions, not how it yields judgments or linguistic descriptions.[6]

According to Berkeley and Gibson, "Why do things look as they do?"

is the central question for a theory of vision if the question is construed as asking about the visual world, not the visual field. And up to a crucial point, to be discussed later, their reasons for stressing this version of the question are much alike. They both tend to assume that an explanation of why the visual field looks as it does can be found in some version of the constancy hypothesis. So a solution to this psychological problem, as opposed to coming up with an account of the underlying physiological mechanisms involved, was pretty much on hand. Of more importance, Berkeley and Gibson each make much of the fact that it is our experience of the visual world that is significant for behavior. This leads them both to emphasize the inseparability of seeing and doing. A quote from Gibson's last book, *The Ecological Approach to Visual Perception*, highlights this aspect of their agreement.

> The theory of affordances implies that to see things is to see how to get about among them and what to do or not to do with them. If this is true, visual perception serves behavior, and behavior is controlled by perception. The observer who does not move but only stands and looks is not behaving at the moment, it is true, but he cannot help seeing the affordances for behavior in whatever he looks at.[7]

It would seem, then, that Berkeley and Gibson are in accord about the primary function of vision and the primary matter of interest in the study of vision. Their disagreements are over certain more local issues in vision theory, as well as the metaphysical implications they believe their contrasting models entail. I will leave discussion of these metaphysical topics to last and start with what appear to be some differences in their treatments of seeing distance and size.

Distance

In *The Perception of the Visual World*, Gibson proposes to reorient the study of spatial perception away from the dominant Berkeleian approach. Here is how Gibson saw the situation a little more than 40 years ago. "The traditional explanation of vision is that perceiving things depends on first having sensations."[8] "Perception goes beyond the stimuli and is superimposed on sensations."[9] While there had been attempts to treat certain aspects of spatial vision as sensations, the one-point argument seemed to preclude that distance be so understood. "No one ever supposed that depth and distance were simple sensations, and the visual third dimension was and remained a phenomenon which only perception could explain."[10] But Gibson claims that "if a sensory basis for such properties could be discovered in the retinal image . . . the whole intellectual superstructure would fall."[11] It would then be possible "to account for depth and distance . . . without the necessity of supposing a special mental process to supplement the images."[12]

How does Gibson propose to overcome the one-point argument and topple the tradition? His account involves several different theses. First, he claims that there is a kind of distance that is directly represented in the image. While he admits that the one-point argument shows that distance along a line of sight is not seen, he notes that a receding surface, especially that of the ground, is generally displayed in the retinal image. Adherents of the one-point argument, of course, would not dispute this optical fact. The problem for them is to understand how such a two-dimensional display of the ground can give rise to an appreciation of distance in the third dimension. In addition, retinal extent does not correspond with actual physical distance. Depending on whether you are looking across a room or across a football field, different surface extents may project the same-size retinal images. The accompanying sensations of phenomenal extent can no more be identified with our idea of a specific distance than any one of the fluctuating visual field sizes that we experience of an object as we move about can be identified with the idea of the object's physical size.

Gibson's second thesis is an attempt to resolve these difficulties. He claims that it is possible to show that the retinal image of the receding plane can trigger an experience of distance that does not require mental processing. T. G. R. Bower begins a chapter on distance perception of his book *Development in Infancy* with a succinct account of Gibson's strategy.[13] After quoting sections 2 and 3 of Berkeley's *New Theory*, Bower argues:

> Although this view is still encountered . . . it should not have survived the clarifying analysis of Gibson. . . . Gibson pointed out that there are many stimuli that specify distance. Once projected on the two-dimensional retina the stimuli are not themselves three dimensional. However, variations within these stimuli specify variations in distance to a degree of accuracy limited only by the resolving power of the optical system of the eye. We thus see distance as directly as we see color.[14]

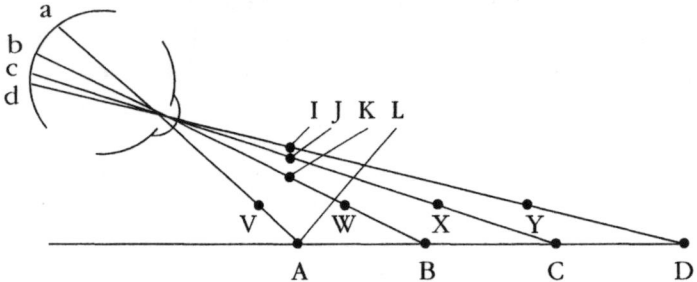

Figure 4.1   *The use and ambiguity of texture gradients in determining distances. The arrays A B C D, I J K L, and V W X Y all project to a b c d.*

The idea seems to be that we can escape the difficulties of the one-point argument by enriching our conception of the stimulus for distance. If instead of treating spatial points individually, as the one-point argument does, the stimulus is taken to be the entire array, then there are patterns in the stimulus array – for example, those due to the texture of the ground – that can directly trigger a distance evaluation (see figure 4.1). When a regularly textured surface (A, B, C, D) recedes from an observer, the distances between the retinal projections (a, b, c, d) of the elements of the texture decrease correspondingly. Gibson's proposal is to take advantage of such relational features of the optic array and treat distance perception much as the non-psychic theorists treat neutral color or color contrast. The existence of these higher-order properties of the stimulus array, Gibson thinks, means that there is no need to postulate intermediate steps of mental processing. Our sensory mechanisms simply respond to stimulus patterns or gradients which enable us to sense distance directly. As the constancy hypothesis maintains, the properties of the visual field may be a reflection of the absolute properties of the stimulus. But Gibson holds that our experience of the visual *world* is also simply a matter of a reaction of the visual system to the properties of the stimulus. A version of the constancy hypothesis holds for the visual world too. The difference is that perception of the visual world is in accord with relative or higher-order properties of the stimulus. It does not depend on the perceiver interpreting or "reading through" the visual field. Perception is not based on prior sensations of the visual field, and these fluctuating sensations should not be understood as the data on which we construct the visual world.

Now it is important to separate several different claims here. One has to do with the richness of the stimulus: whether it contains enough information to specify distance uniquely. Another concerns whether such an enrichment would show that distance perception is direct or immediate. Another still has to do with whether perception is based on sensation.[15] In the particular limited case illustrated in figure 4.1, the answer to the first question is "no." Without additional constraints, it fails to meet head on an important aspect of the one-point argument. For nothing in the situation described, by itself provides a sufficient basis for determining the actual distance. If the points were distributed in space as illustrated by I, J, K, L, in figure 4.1, they would project the same retinal stimulus as the points A, B, C, D.[16] What is more, even with the assumptions that the texture is regular and that the texture gradient itself is used to inform us that the points all lie along a plane parallel to the ground, the stimulus will not provide *absolute* distance information (i.e., how far off in space the points are from the perceiver). The arrangement of points V, W, X, Y indicates why this is so. Without additional assumptions or input there is not enough information in this stimulus to determine the absolute distance. The units of texture can be used to provide a distance scale, but this will remain a relative measure of distance unless the size of the units of texture is known.[17]

Gibson and his followers have become increasingly sensitive to these limitations of static stimuli and have for years stressed the crucial importance of information that depends on movement. Such additional stimulus information can specify the layout more accurately and, if expanded sufficiently, might correlate uniquely with a given spatial arrangement.[18]

Clearly Gibson's pioneering work in calling attention to the importance of surfaces or the terrain, along with his efforts to expand our understanding of the information available to the perceiver by including texture gradients and other ratios or invariants, is a major achievement. It is an achievement that serves to undermine those theories of vision that depend on the assumption that the data available for spatial perception are much more scanty. I have argued, however, that Berkeley, at least, does not claim that the stimulus for distance is necessarily ambiguous and that the main thrust of Berkeley's theory does not depend on this sort of impoverishment assumption. The oculomotor cues of convergence and accommodation are not ambiguous in the way that pictorial cues are. And were the properties of light such that brightness or color varied directly with distance, they might each provide an unambiguous, *strictly visual* basis for assessing distance. Nevertheless, for Berkeley this would not mean that distance perception is immediate or that spatial distance, in and of itself, is a property of our visual experience. It would only show that there are some visual cues to distance capable of providing un- ambiguous data about how far off things are. It would not follow from this that ideas of "brightness" or "color" should themselves be considered "distance" ideas.[19]

Gibson seems to have got Berkeley wrong, or only partly right, on a further important matter. In *The Ecological Approach to Visual Perception*, after presenting reasons for rejecting the one-point argument, Gibson con- cludes: "Distance therefore is *not* a line end-wise to the eye as Bishop Berkeley thought. To think so is to confuse abstract geometrical space with the living space of the environment. It is to confuse the Z-axis of a Cartesian coordinate system with the number of paces along the ground to a fixed object."[20] This confusion, though, is not easily attributed to Berkeley. A major goal of the *New Theory* is to provide an understanding of distance perception in terms of something like paces or ideas of move- ment, so as not to have to appeal to abstract ideas of space. Berkeley takes himself to be significantly at odds with other philosophers and the optic writers on this very issue.

Has Gibson's reconception of the stimuli for distance perception never- theless served to undermine the traditional paradigm of space perception? Surely his stress on the importance of the ground or surface distances versus line-of-sight distances and his discovery of a wide range of stimuli that contain information about the spatial layout have undermined some of the empirical claims and assumptions of the dominant tradition. But in doing so, has not Gibson also shown that distance perception is really immediate or direct? There is no one satisfactory answer to this question, I think. For the question itself is vague and subject to alternative interpretations, which range from issues having empirical content to others that seem more a quibble over terminology. Indeed, much of this debate mirrors our story in chapter 3 of the controversy concerning inference.

At the more empirical end of the direct – indirect dispute may be found, among others, questions about whether particular features of dis- tance perception are learned or innate or whether expectations and con- scious propositional knowledge can affect what we see.[21] At the other extreme, the debate turns into some version of "Can we really see* dis- tance?" This epistemological question, I have argued, has little connec- tion with substantive empirical issues in the theory of vision. Between these extremes are a set of questions with varying degrees of clarity and empirical or theoretical import. On some accounts, the problem of direct perception is viewed primarily as a dispute over the role that sensations or visual fields play in determining distance. On other accounts, the issue turns on whether the stimulus for distance is rich or impoverished. On still others, the main question concerns the kind of processing that goes on and whether it is organic (hence direct) rather than mental or psychological (hence indirect). I have covered much of this territory in chapter 3. I will discuss these issues as they apply specifically to Gibson later on in this chapter.

Size

What constitutes the (or a) Gibsonian theory of size perception is not totally clear. One view of what is most important in Gibson's work on seeing magnitude concerns his ideas about the role and sufficiency of ratios, gradients, or other higher-order stimulus properties. Gibson argues, for example, that the texture elements of a surface described above provide a means for evaluating size. Each texture unit can be thought of as a unit of size, and the size of an object may be determined by the number of texture units it takes up. Although the retinal image of an object decreases in size with distance, the retinal projections of the units of texture also decrease with distance. An object or objects of the same size will occupy the same number of texture units regardless of their distance from the observer (see Figure 4.2). Object size can be scaled in terms of texture units. Thus, Gibson says, size can be determined directly, without having to take distance into account.

This aspect of the Gibsonian approach to size perception faces several difficulties. First, there are various empirical findings that some theorists believe weigh against the claim that perceivers make crucial use of texture units in evaluating size. Second, the simple version of the model only works for evaluating the size of objects or those parts of objects actually lying on the textured surface. For objects or their parts rising from the ground, the number of texture units occluded from sight will be a function not only of the object's size but also of the distance and slope of the object relative to the observer. The number of units that such an object occludes from sight is not the same as the number of units that the object takes up where it makes contact with the surface. Were the slabs in figure

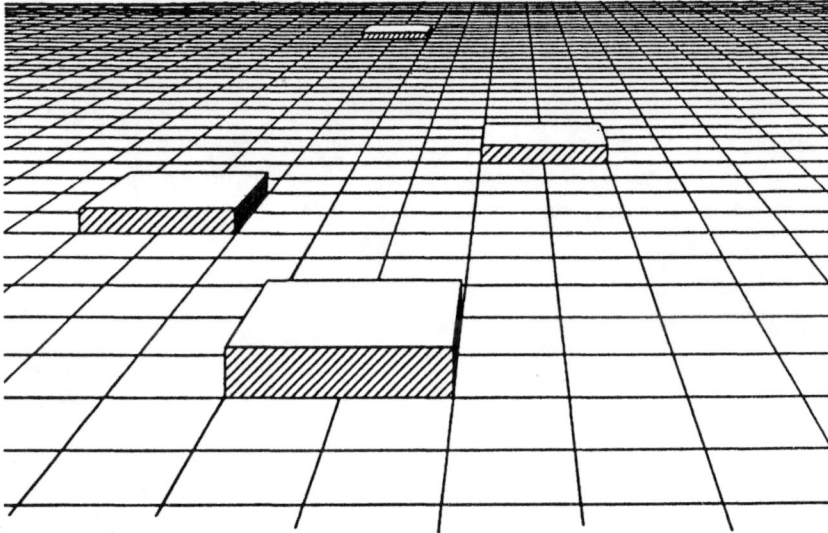

Figure 4.2   *The size of an object can be evaluated in terms of the number of texture units it occupies.*

4.2 standing on their edges, the closer slabs would occlude fewer units of background texture than the more distant ones. Finally, as presented, the theory provides only for "relative," not specific, measures of size. We might be able to account in this way for size constancy, comparative size evaluations, or size relative to the texture units. What would remain to be explained is our ability to tell how big an object is in more absolute terms, especially in terms appropriate to guide behavior.[22] In order to determine this fuller evaluation of size, we need additional information; namely, we need to know the size of the texture units or something equivalent. It is a version of the calibration problem all over again.

How might some of these latter difficulties be handled within a Gibsonian framework? Gibson's student W. C. Purdy offers a possible solution.[23] Purdy's model, in its simplest form, is diagrammed in figure 4.3. Purdy shows that the ground distance, d_1, can be computed from information about the optical slant (the angle β formed by the intersection of a line from the eye to the surface), plus a measure of the distance, d_2, from eye level to the ground. The expanse from the eye to the ground need not, and often is not, represented in the retinal image. Its value must be assumed or determined separately. Purdy demonstrates

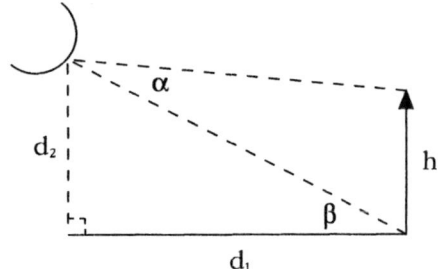

Figure 4.3 *Purdy's model. The information available for determining the ground distance* d *and the size* h.

that the value of the optical slant, though, is derivable from information concerning the texture gradient. It is then easy to prove that with this same value for the optical slant and with a measure of the visual angle α, the size of an object, h, situated on a plane perpendicular to the line of sight can be calculated.

Purdy's solution to the problem of size evaluation may be thought of as a kind of two-angle triangulation formula. It differs from those discussed in chapter 2 in that Purdy's model relies on the assumption that d_1 and d_2 form a right angle. Like the standard presentations of the TAD model, it tends to bury in this assumption the fact that the distance, or, as I would just as soon call it, the "size" d_1 cannot be determined with values for only one angle and a single distance. In turn, this or an equivalent right-angle assumption is needed if the computation of d_1 and the subsequent computation of h are to go through. What is importantly different in Purdy's model is that neither d_1 nor d_2 is a line-of-sight distance, a measure that Gibsonians and others find suspect.[24] The model does presume, though, that the perceiver somehow has an appreciation, perhaps kinesthetic, of d_2, the distance between eye level and the ground. And the model, as presented, does require information concerning the optical slant, which is comparable here to a line-of-sight intersection. The need for a measure of the optical slant is thought unproblematic, since it can be computed from the texture gradient.

Suppose, then, that some version of Purdy's Gibsonian-influenced analysis is correct and can be used to supplement the simpler Gibsonian account discussed initially. Would this provide support for the claim that size perception is direct? For many theorists, any account that literally depended on the type of calculations that Purdy describes would, like the standard TAD models, be considered a paradigm case of inferential or non-direct perception. It would be considered indirect because it postulates a kind of computational processing that these theorists deem to be mental or psychological. The fact that the model appeals to higher-order stimulus variables, avoids using line-of-sight distances, and takes seriously Gibson's ground theory approach to evaluating spatial layout would not affect this point. However, I will leave further probing of the issue of direct versus indirect size perception aside for now.[25]

Instead, I wish to discuss briefly where things stand with regard to several of the other issues raised in chapter 2. Like the earlier models, Purdy's formulas depend on information that varies as a function of the distance and slant of the spatial extent whose size is to be measured. Purdy's model also treats ground distances differently from size. In its simple form, moreover, it provides size evaluations only for objects that lie on a fronto-parallel plane. The seriousness of these considerations for a general theory of size perception is again underscored once the analysis ceases to be restricted to two-dimensional poles, arrows, or ground distances on fronto-parallel or sagittal planes, and attempts to encompass ordinary, especially three-dimensional, objects whose surfaces vary continuously in slant and distance from the observer (e.g., a tree together with its branches, an automobile pointing toward us, or a globe). In addition, if Purdy's model is to be ecologically realistic, it must allow that a good many of the objects that we see throughout the day (e.g., those on my desk or dining room table), are not in direct contact with the ground and do not bear any simple relation to any single ground distance. Augmenting Purdy's model so that it can be applied to a fuller range of objects, however, raises many of the very same questions noted in chapter 2, questions concerning which size evaluations the model claims are actually computed, whether the rich information needed for such computations might render the derivation of H values superfluous, and so forth. For nothing in those previous arguments depended crucially on the fact that the distances used were line-of-sight distances rather than measures that reflect or are more dependent on surface textures and ground distances.

Compared with the TAD models reviewed earlier, Purdy's theory has some advantages. In particular, the only distance measure really required to calculate size is the height of the eye from the ground, and it might seem to be less of a problem accounting for our having an absolute measure of this distance than for our having absolute measures of line-of-sight distances. Further, a measure of this eye-to-ground distance is not needed where the task requires only comparative size evaluations or evaluations relativized to d_2 as a constant scale factor.

A few final points concerning chapter 2 and Gibson's own simpler relational model of size perception are worth mentioning. Like Berkeley, Gibson claims that the cues or variables for size perception are the same as those for distance. Texture gradients serve to scale both size and distance. Gibson cites this dual function of gradients to explain why judgments of size and distance tend to go together or are coupled, as proponents of the Invariance Hypothesis might claim. Gibson emphasizes this linkage by arguing that in ordinary vision we do not perceive size per se but always *size-at-a-distance*. We see the size of an object as so many texture units, at so many texture units of distance. I am greatly in sympathy with Gibson's employment of the locution "size-at-a-distance" to remind us that distance is just size between two points, and vice versa, that size is just distance between two points. In chapter 2, in fact, I went on to speculate that the supposed coupling of size and distance might simply be a reflection of the interchangeability of these properties. In this, I believe that my criticism of the TAD model is of a piece with Gibson's conception of size evaluation and in accord with some of his later remarks challenging the usual distinction between distance and size.[26] Where I think the "size-at-a-distance" locution can be misleading, though, is in suggesting that objects have a perceptual size at a distance. The original problem with the TAD theory, as examined in chapter 2, was that for many, if not most, objects, there is no single distance at which it makes good sense to locate the entire (linear) extent of an object. The empirical limitation of assuming such a unique distance, I claimed, is obscured by the practice of many theorists of defining "size" as separation on a fronto-parallel plane and "distance" as separation on a sagittal plane and of testing size perception using only two-dimensional objects perpendicular to the ground and the line of sight.

Direct Perception

In a very controversial and frequently cited paper, Jerry Fodor and Zenon Pylyshyn launched a broad general challenge to the Gibsonian theme that perception is direct and not inferential.[27] As one might expect, Gibson's followers remain unconvinced.[28] My own view is that in many of its guises this dispute is lacking in substance. Moreover, in those areas where substantive issues are at stake, the arguments for and against the Fodor and Pylyshyn critique of direct perception are not very telling. This is a reflection of the fact that these debates turn less on the empirical theory of vision adopted than on how the theory is characterized. And here, I submit again, the disputes retrace those about inference considered in chapter 3. A quick review of Fodor and Pylyshyn's paper can serve to indicate the major similarities between the issues discussed in chapter 3 and our present concerns.[29]

One of Fodor and Pylyshyn's main criticisms of Gibson depends on an argument akin to some found in epistemological defenses of visual inference.[30] Fodor and Pylyshyn maintain that there is an important asymmetry between the properties of light and the properties of the environmental layout, which shows that it is the former, not the latter, that can properly be said to be "picked up." The asymmetry they spell out is one of causal dependence or priority. Presented with an appropriately organized array of light, a person will perceive a spatial layout even if the stimulus is artificially produced and no real environment of that kind is the source of the array. Conversely, given a spatial layout, if the light that it ordinarily reflects is distorted or withheld, the person will not see how things are in the environment. Fodor and Pylyshyn offer a very simple and convincing proof of this last point. Turn out the lights, and nothing will be perceived. Fodor and Pylyshyn argue that this causal asymmetry proves that of the two it must be the properties of light which are "picked up," not the properties of the environment.

Now this causal dependence of vision on light, although an empirical finding, is not likely to be disputed, and its truth would seem compatible with any reasonable account of vision. The question, then, is whether considerations this sort show that only properties of light, and not environmental properties, can be picked up or sensed. The significance of the Fodor and Pylyshyn asymmetry for establishing this thesis, however, is blunted once it is recognized that a claim similar to theirs might be made about the properties of light too. Retinal stimuli, after all, initiate a chain of neural events that bear an asymmetric relation to the properties of the light array. Produce these subsequent neural impulses directly, a bit in from the retina, and the organism will have visual experience without actually being stimulated by light. In earlier times the same point might have been made by appealing to a Cartesian demon. Conversely, stimulate the retina but interrupt the flow of neural impulses a few steps in, and the organism will see nothing. There is, then, a causal asymmetry between the properties of light and the neural impulses that they may trigger. Since all theories of vision allow that there is a good deal of necessary neural processing that goes on beyond the retina, the mere existence of a causal asymmetry between the spatial layout and the light array would not seem a sufficient basis for determining what can or cannot be picked up.

Fodor and Pylyshyn recognize that if the claim that vision depends on inference is to make full sense, it is necessary to distinguish the data for vision from the perceptions or hypotheses which they claim are derived from this evidence. They attempt to do this by introducing the idea of a "transducer." The output of processes of transduction is what is given to the visual system as data; the operations that process this data are the cognitive steps described as inference. Making this distinction depends, however, on there being an unproblematic specification of the notion of "transduction." As Fodor and Pylyshyn admit, there is no one, agreed-upon definition of this concept. They note, in fact, that their opponents might argue that the organism or visual system as a whole is a transducer. On this construal, the end state, the perception, is simply transduced, and there would be no place for inference to do any work. In order to counter this response, Fodor and Pylyshyn offer their own, more restrictive definition of "transduction."

Their characterization of transduction is a little complex, and it relies on some problematic claims about projectible versus non-projectible properties, along with other debatable assumptions. But the details of their analysis need not concern us. For suppose that the Fodor and Pylyshyn definition of "transduction" is accepted; the question remains as to why the output of transduction is to be deemed "data" and the processing of this output "inference." The intuition seems to be that the doings of transducers are not "mental" or "psychological" operations, whereas the subsequent processing is. The soundness of this claim rests, in turn, on a useful specification of what the significant difference is between purely "physiological" processing and that which is "psychic" or "cognitive." In chapter 3 I expressed qualms about there being a particular need and firm way to make this distinction.

Gibson, in any case, does not doubt that the workings of the visual system depend on rich neurological processing. He denies, however, that these operations are properly characterized in either traditional mentalistic terms or, in what he sees as their contemporary substitute, an information-processing vocabulary. I find none too clear Gibson's own attempts to spell out the distinction between mentalist and non-mentalist models and to explain why the distinction is important. In different places Gibson seems to associate his notion of the "mental" with versions of each of the criteria for inference considered in chapter 3. At times the mental is loosely characterized along the lines of "folk psychology." Perception is not direct if it depends on knowledge of the world or if it is "mediated by assumptions, preconceptions, expectations, mental images, or any of a dozen other hypothetical mediators."[31] At times the notion of a "mental mediator" extends beyond the domain of folk psychology to include *any* state said to have representational status. But then Gibson and Gibsonians often construe representational states quite narrowly, identifying them with states that employ concepts or symbols of the sort that we use in our everyday intellectual endeavors.[32] Elsewhere, though, the notion of a "representational state" is much more widely conceived to include any item that may be thought of as containing information. Numerous other commentators and followers explicate Gibson's view of mental representation as falling between these two extremes.

Gary Hatfield's paper entitled "Gibsonian Representation and Connectionist Symbol-Processing: Prospects for Unification" is an instructive example of a recent attempt to clarify and defend the anti-mentalistic commitments of the Gibsonian paradigm.[33] Hatfield argues that it is possible to be a Gibsonian and allow for a wide range of computations by the visual system, as long it is not assumed that the perceiver makes use of "symbolic" representations. Accordingly, Hatfield cites developments in connectionist models of cognition as a way to talk about complex computations and information processing without characterizing these operations in the sort of symbolic terminology that, for him, would make perception inferential, not direct.

Approaches like Hatfield's depend, of course, on how one distinguishes symbolic from nonsymbolic representations and on how one conceives of the workings of connectionist models – whether they "really" are only models of the mechanisms that *implement* psychological operations, and whether in the end connectionist models "really" do avoid making use of symbolic representations.[34] The significance of Hatfield's analysis also depends crucially on how strong a link one assumes there is between the purported use of symbolic representations and an appropriate concept of the "mental." It would appear that the importance to a Gibsonian of establishing the asymbolic nature of visual processing would be much attenuated if, like Fodor, the theorist admits that ascriptions of content or intentionality to a state do not entail that the state is psychological in the way that beliefs and desires are.[35] For surely it has been the need to appeal to such fuller-bodied psychological states that champions of direct perception have most wished to deny when claiming that vision does not involve mental states and processing.

I am not arguing here that questions concerning connectionist models of learning, neurological architecture, and cognitive activities necessarily lack empirical or theoretical significance. I believe, nonetheless, that debates about connectionism and the mental, like the related controversies over the boundaries of the intentional or the psychological, are typically carried out on a level of abstraction that is far removed from specific studies and findings in the theory of vision. This general point is apparent in Fodor and Pylyshyn's fast and loose use of the notion of "visual inference." The notion is characterized mainly in negative terms, as whatever goes on that is not transduction. For Fodor and Pylyshyn, once they establish that something is given as data by transduction, nearly anything that happens to it beyond that point is described as inference. Thus, as in places they seem to allow, their version of the thesis that vision is inferential would appear compatible with an enormous range of conflicting theories of spatial perception, including many of a Gibsonian stripe. Just as Fodor and Pylyshyn correctly claim that Gibson's idea of "pickup" is not sufficiently constrained, so their own notion of "inference" is almost totally unconstrained. The quite global type of arguments that Fodor, Pylyshyn and others put forth about asymmetries, transduction, information pickup, and the like go through (or fail) pretty much independent of most of the empirical and theoretical issues that separate Gibsonian and conflicting accounts of visual phenomena.

Agreeing with Fodor and Pylyshyn that vision is based on inference would seem to leave open, for instance, all the more substantive empirical issues recounted in chapter 3 concerning competing versions of how we perceive a cup. More generally, Fodor and Pylyshyn's analysis is also compatible with a wide variety of processing models. As we have seen, there are some significant differences between Gibsonian accounts of size perception and the traditional TAD model. Likewise, there are major differences between taking-account-of-slant models of shape recognition and certain Gibsonian approaches. The former postulate that the visual system combines distinct information about slant with information about the shape of the retinal image to compute the objective shape. The latter claim that there are invariant relations between an object and its environment that specify shape-at-a-slant. On the Gibsonian account, there supposedly is no need for independent representations of slant and retinal shape or for computations over these representations to determine objective shape.[36] Yet all these models might be said to involve inference if the Fodor and Pylyshyn viewpoint is adopted.

Accepting Fodor and Pylyshyn's claim that vision depends on inference also leaves open many of the most general and controversial questions in vision theory, such as: (1) Do conscious sensations play a role in perception? (2) Are aspects of spatial perception the result of innate constraints? (3) Under what circumstances might there be enough information in the stimulus array to determine the layout uniquely? (4) Are the states and processes of basic spatial perception modular, cognitively impenetrable, or stimulus driven? (5) Does perception depend on or result in egocentric versus environment-centered specifications of the layout?

Fodor and Pylyshyn's thesis that vision is based on inference is not so much false as lacking in consequence for the study of vision. The same holds for most of the counterclaims made by those who maintain that perception is direct. My point, then, is not that it is impossible to draw such a distinction. My concerns are more about the need and real significance of doing so. I believe that a major reason why the arguments concerning inference are assumed to have more substance than they do is the failure to appreciate the range and optionality of the given – supplementation dichotomy explored in chapter 3. The parallels are obvious. For example, if "transduction" is defined in Fodor and Pylyshyn's way, then Y is given, and Z is supplemented by inference. Define "transduction" differently, and X is given, and Y supplemented. Debates about *the* proper definition of transduction, in turn, usually depend on a supposition or intuition that there is a single, natural, and fixed place to draw the line between where "nature's lawlike input" ends and where our "mental," "psychological," or "intentional" supplementation begins.

Realism and Metaphysics

I have noted several times that merely enriching the notion of "stimulus" and allowing for higher-order stimulus properties will not show that perception is non-inferential or immediate on a wide variety of construals of these notions. People can and have argued that such relational or gradient properties of the stimulus should simply be treated as additional cues. The fact that these cues are higher-order stimulus features and may provide unambiguous information would not entail that perception is direct. Perception, it is claimed, still depends on "interpreting" the cues. The Gibsonian response to this argument is that the traditional approach goes wrong at just the point at which it conceptualizes these features of the light array as *cues*. Being sensitive to the higher-level invariant features of the stimulus array is not to sense "signs" of the environment, but to sense spatial properties of the environment themselves. To resonate with or be attuned to the invariants is to see the environment directly. It is not a matter of sensing an intermediary, something that merely "stands for" what we see.

Sometimes those who reject this Gibsonian analysis argue that in principle there cannot be an identification of environmental properties with the features of the stimulus. They claim, therefore, that on a priori grounds it follows that spatial perception cannot be direct. So conceived, the debate over direct perception may be understood to hinge on resolving some tricky metaphysical, epistemological, and linguistic problems about property identity, individuation, and reference. This is a swamp of issues that it is best to avoid, and I think, by and large, that we can. For many of the controversies over vision will not go away even if we suppose that the invariants are identical to, or essential properties of, our spatial environment in the way it is claimed that H_2O is identical with or essential to something being water. To appreciate this, consider how the issues might play out in the very case of water. Does detecting or picking up water entail detecting or picking up H_2O? There is a well-known ambiguity in such questions, roughly that between *de dicto* and *de re* construals (or, as it is sometimes characterized, the difference between the notions "seeing as" and "seeing"). In the *de dicto* sense, someone may detect or pick up that the stuff is water or is labeled "water" without being aware that it is H_2O. In the *de re* sense of "detect" or "pick up," it is a matter of definition that if water $= H_2O$, then to detect or pick up water is to detect or pick up H_2O. Either way, on this specific issue, there seems to be no interestingly disputable point about vision at stake. Whichever empirical theory of vision is adopted, it would seem possible to allow room within it for both a *de dicto* and *de re* sense of detection.[37]

Viewing the direct perception issue as one that depends on an identity of the invariants or other properties of the light array with properties of the environment also does not appear to jibe with Gibson's own intentions.

Gibson says over and over again that the properties of the light array are not themselves to be identified with the environmental properties that we see. They are, he says, *lawlike* correlates of these environmental properties; they are causally related to them. Gibson talks as though the lawlike nature of these correlations is important. He thinks that establishing such a causal link between the invariants and the correlated spatial properties shows that these features of the light array are not "signs" or "symbols" for the layout. They are not like the arbitrary words of a language that we have to learn to interpret. It is a matter of convention that "cat" denotes cats and "dog" denotes dogs. It is a lawlike fact of physics or optics or ecological optics that properties of the light array vary with the environment in the ways they do. To appreciate these lawlike correlations is to get things right about the way in which the world is independent of any human or mental construction. Gibson is willing to admit that the empiricists may be correct in claiming that various aspects of perception require learning. But, he says, this does not mean that in learning to detect and appreciate the invariants of the light array we are seeing signs and are thus a step removed from what is "out there." We are, instead, becoming better attuned to the mind-independent lawlike features of reality.

How this all bears on the issue of direct versus indirect theories of vision is not too easy to sort out. For example, Berkeley's allegiance to a language theory of vision does not mean that he thinks that the connections between visual signs and their referents is not lawlike. These correlations, for Berkeley, are not a matter of human device or desire. The visual language is the language of nature or God.[38] Berkeley uses the language analogy to emphasize his claim that we cannot tell by a priori reason or by similarity what is correlated with what. Berkeley does not argue that the correlations are a matter of human or nonnatural convention.

At the same time, establishing the significance of Gibson's own claim that the features of the light array bear a lawlike relation to the spatial layout is not without its problems. According to Peirce's well-known theory of signs, for example, smoke may be considered a sign for fire, although a causal relationship exists between them. Signs that bear such a connection to their referents are called "indices," and it is this causal relationship that is said to distinguish indices from arbitrary symbols like "cat" and "dog." Still, both indices and symbols are taken by Peirce to be signs. What is more, attempts to naturalize the intentional aspects of sign use have led many theorists to try to give a causal twist to their analyses of symbols. It is argued that symbols too bear causal relationships to their referents, and it is this that helps to determine a symbol's semantic status.[39] So agreeing with Gibson that the link between features of the light array and the features of the environment they specify is causal may not preclude understanding them as bearing a semantic or intentional sign relation.[40] Would the adoption of a causal or lawlike analysis of the sign relation entail, then, that vision "really" is indirect or based on inference? What goes around comes around.

But doesn't Gibson's work showing that there are invariant features of the light array capable of specifying the layout undercut a crucial assumption of the traditional paradigm? A central argument employed by Berkeley and other proponents of indirect perception depends on the claim that whereas our subjective visual experience fluctuates, our ideas and perceptions of the physical environment are stable. The retinal and phenomenal size and shape of a cup may change continually as we move about, but we see and attribute to the cup a single objective size and shape. Therefore, it is claimed, our ideas or concepts of the cup's constant physical size and shape cannot be identified with any of its variable phenomenal sizes and shapes. We cannot, in principle, immediately see the real size and shape of the cup, or for that matter the physical size and shape of any object.

Evaluating the force of Gibson's ideas in challenging this line of argument requires distinguishing two issues, one more empirical, the other more philosophical. Gibson, we have seen, allows for a distinction between the visual field and the visual world; he also allows that the visual field fluctuates, or is not constant, compared to our perceptual evaluations. But he denies that experience of a stable visual world depends on, or is the result of, interpreting variable visual sensations. According to Gibson, there is no need to account for how we are able to have constant ideas of the environment, given the variability in the stimulus, because there is an important constancy in the stimulus itself. Whereas the absolute properties of the light array fluctuate with movement or change in orientation, the higher-order properties, those that specify the perceived environment or visual world, are invariant. Differences in the absolute properties of the stimulus may account for some of the variable properties of the visual field, as the older constancy hypothesis maintains; but, according to Gibson, a richer version of the constancy hypothesis holds for the visual world. The whole problem of accounting for constancy amid phenomenal instability is a bogus one. We are forced to claim that vision is indirect only if we assume that perception is based on fluctuating visual field sensations in the way that the traditional paradigm maintains. Once this faulty assumption is abandoned, it is no longer necessary to deny that perception of the constant features of the world is direct.

It is in going from the first to the second clause of this last sentence that the issue begins to drift from the empirical to the philosophical. The question of whether perception is a two-stage process in which perceptions are derived from sensations would seem to have some empirical import. How much and what import it has, though, is itself a function of the meaning given to the concepts "sensation," "perception," and "based on sensations." If sensations are understood as not requiring any conscious display (e.g., sensations may be unconscious representations of features of the retinal image), then the sensation − perception distinction takes on a testably different guise than if consciousness is required. The empirical split between Gibsonians and other theorists may then be primarily over which or what kinds of properties of the light array are registered. The empirical significance of Gibson's denial that perception is based on sensation would be different, however, if the issue is fought out more broadly in terms of whether registering or picking up information of any sort requires *symbolic* representations. And experimental data would be even less relevant if what is at stake is whether the employment of symbols entails that the states are cognitive, psychological, mental, or intentional.

The issues become most metaphysical and devoid of empirical content when the split turns on questions of property identity, the nature of reality and assumptions about what we may correctly be said to really see*. For suppose Gibson is right, and there are invariants in the light array that are correlated in a lawlike manner (or are even theoretically identical) with properties of the spatial layout. Does this mean that we can see* these properties of the environment in and of themselves? Or suppose Gibson is wrong, and there are no constant stimulus features corresponding to the layout, or that these stable higher-order stimulus properties do not specify the environment uniquely. Would that mean that we do not see* the world, or do not see* it as it is? These questions by now sound familiar, and I would not think of attempting to answer them.

But what of the ultimate metaphysical issue that separates Berkeley and Gibson? Berkeley uses his work on vision to support idealism, while Gibson argues that adoption of his approach to the theory of vision goes to establish a realist doctrine. I have argued elsewhere that the realist thesis of a world ready-made, independent of our contribution, is no more tenable than the idea that the world is whatever we fancy it to be.[41] Further, a radical subjectivist thesis is no part of Berkeley's idealism. Veridical perception and correct theories of the world are not matters of wishing making them so. For Berkeley, too, there is a distinction between the subjective and the objective. Finally, once Berkeley gives up identifying the real exclusively with the tangible and takes on a more phenomenalistic ontology, he can grant that we see physical reality in the only sense that he is willing to assign to the notion of "physical reality."

At the same time, I do not see how accepting the empirical content of a Gibsonian theory of perception entails any strong realist position concerning a ready-made, mind-independent world to which our true theories or veridical perceptions correspond. As for the ontological issues that may remain, the view to which I myself am attracted is an ecumenical "irrealist" position.[42] It is a standpoint that questions the sense, value, or need of taking sides in most of these metaphysical controversies. For those like Berkeley and Gibson who do find issues about the nature of reality pressing, the first step would be to specify these seemingly conflicting ontological doctrines in a clear non-tendentious manner. This, by itself, is no easy task. My bet, however, is that when this is accomplished, it will become even more apparent that the choice between the doctrines depends little on any substantive, currently studied issue in the theory of vision. It will depend on philosophical views about truth and the essence of reality, epistemological commitments about what can be "really" seen*, and the relationships presumed to exist among these positions.

In many places Gibson expresses the fear that if vision is conceived of as indirect or based on inference or modeled in the information-processing idiom, it will lead to dualism. There will be the environment and our movements in it that are "physical" and perception and perceptual operations that are "mental."[43] But these fears, however bothersome, are misguided. After all, the metaphysics that Berkeley himself ends up promoting rejects dualism, albeit in favor of a nonmaterialist ontology. Such an immaterialist escape from Gibson's worries undoubtedly conflicts with current materialist tendencies in philosophy and science, and few would be happy if it were the only option. Clearly it is not. It is commonplace these days that it is possible to talk about neural events in mentalistic terms without that entailing acceptance of a Cartesian substance dualism of mind and body. Likewise, characterizing states and transitions of the visual system in information-processing terms need not imply any scary form of anti-materialism. On many interpretations of "information processing," the model may be applied naturally to the workings of our kidneys or heart, or for that matter to thermometers and hand-held calculators, without carrying a commitment to there being anything peculiarly nonmaterial about the domain. It would seem that serious work in the theory of vision can best proceed by letting these grander metaphysical issues float free on their own.

Notes

1 See Edward Reed, *James J. Gibson and the Psychology of Perception* (Yale University Press, New Haven, Conn., 1988). Throughout this intellectual biography of Gibson, Reed makes the case not only that have critics misunderstood Gibson, but also that Gibson's students and followers have failed to get crucial notions and points correct.

2 I remind those who may feel that any such comparison is anachronistic of the genesis of this book, in a course that used the *New Theory* as a springboard for exploring contemporary problems in the study of perception. Again, my interest is more in exploring themes in vision theory than in the exegesis of individual positions.

3 Kurt Koffka, *Principles of Gestalt Psychology* (Harcourt, Brace and World, New York, 1935), ch. 3.

4 Questions regarding whether Berkeley is best understood as being a phenomenalist, and if so, what kind, are controversial issues in Berkeley scholarship that must be left aside here.

5 James J. Gibson, *The Perception of the Visual World* (Houghton Mifflin, Boston, 1950), esp. ch. 3. In subsequent works Gibson alters and revises his views about the nature of this distinction, further distancing his position from the more standard accounts of the sensation – perception dichotomy.

6 For more on Gibson's position and some conflicting interpretations of it, see Thomas Natsoulas, "'Why Do Things Look As They Do?' Some Gibsonian Answers to Koffka's Question," *Philosophical Psychology*, 4 (1991), pp. 183–202.

The gap between Gibson's position and that of Berkeley or Helmholtz is perhaps narrower than it might seem when one takes into account that Berkeley and Helmholtz both sought to distinguish and separate the workings of the visual system from the higher-level intellectual doings of the mind. See chapter 3 on their construals of the differences between suggestion (or unconscious inference) and symbolic scientific reasoning.

7   James J. Gibson, *The Ecological Approach to Visual Perception* (Houghton Mifflin, Boston, 1979), p. 223.

8   Ibid., p. 12.

9   Ibid., p. 13.

10 Ibid., pp. 15–16.

11 Ibid., p. 12.

12 Ibid., p. 116.

13 T. G. R. Bower, *Development in Infancy* (W. H. Freeman, San Francisco, 1974), ch. 4.

14 Ibid., p. 66. Gibson offers a quite similar, even more succinct summary of his many replies to Berkeley in his *Ecological Approach*, p. 117.

15 Of course, the last two issues coalesce if the claim of direct perception is equated with a denial of the claim that perceptions are derived from sensations.

16 Gibson is aware of the issue and discusses the comparable problem of determining where an object makes contact with the ground. He in fact might predict that in the case of I, J, K, L, the display would be mistakenly perceived as a surface running out in space like A, B, C, D. This, however, is not the same as a claim that the texture gradient of the optic array corresponds uniquely to a single physical layout.

17 I discuss some ways in which this might be done in the section on size that follows.

18 One of the bones of contention between Gibsonians and computational theorists has been over this issue of uniqueness. Many computationalists think it important to emphasize that even when higher-order stimulus properties are included, there will not be enough information to specify the layout uniquely unless the visual system comes to the data with constraints or assumptions. See also the discussions at the end of chapter 1 and later in this chapter on the need for a calibration scheme.

19 In fact, aerial perspective, the diminution of brightness with distance, is typically treated in the perception literature as a cue to distance and not as a "distance" idea. It should also be mentioned that Gibson does not deny that the more standardly cited cues like perspective and disparity affect distance perception. Instead, he reconstrues these cues as various kinds of gradients. Binocular retinal disparity, being only one among a larger set of gradients, does not assume for Gibsonians the special role that it has been assigned by most other visual theorists and by other critics of Berkeley.

20 Gibson, *Ecological Approach*, p. 117.

21 Gibson himself does not equate "direct" with "unlearned." For Gibson, learning may be required before we become able to detect and appreciate higher-order stimulus properties, but once learning has taken place, the processing is said to be direct. Many theorists, however, continue to accept

some version of Helmholtz's doctrine that if a phenomenon can be affected by learning, it cannot be understood as a sensation.

22   For more on these lines of criticism, see Irvin Rock, *An Introduction to Perception* (Macmillan, New York, 1975), ch. 2, and *The Logic of Perception* (MIT Press, Cambridge, Mass., 1983), pp. 249ff.

23   I am relying here primarily on presentations of Purdy's work by H. A. Sedgwick, especially "The Geometry of Spatial Layout in Pictorial Representation," in *The Perception of Pictures*, ed. Margaret Hagen (Academic Press, New York, 1980), pp. 33–90. This paper also contains an account of Sedgwick's Gibsonian-inspired horizon theory of size evaluation. It would take us too far afield to examine Sedgwick's own intriguing proposals, although many of the puzzles and problems about size considered in chapter 2 and discussed in this chapter have a bearing on his model as well.

24   Such line-of-sight distance measures are, nonetheless, recoverable from the available data.

25   For discussion of some related issues concerning size evaluation and direct perception, see Julian Hochberg, "Higher-Order Stimuli and Inter-Response Coupling in the Perception of the Visual World," in *Perception: Essays in Honor of J. J. Gibson*, ed. R. B. MacLeod and H. L. Pick (Cornell University Press, Ithaca, N.Y., 1974), pp. 17–39.

26   See, e.g., Gibson, *Ecological Approach*, pp. 160ff.

27   Jerry Fodor and Zenon Pylyshyn, "How Direct is Perception? Some Reflections on Gibson's 'Ecological Approach,'" *Cognition*, 9 (1981), pp. 139–96.

28   See, e.g., M. T. Turvey, R. E. Shaw, E. S. Reed and W. M. Mace, "Ecological Laws of Perceiving and Acting: In Reply to Fodor and Pylyshyn (1981)," Cognition, 9 (1981), pp. 237–304, and Reed, *Gibson and the Psychology of Perception*.

29   My discussion of Fodor and Pylyshyn's paper is aimed not at refuting their various criticisms of Gibson but at exploring the significance and implications of their challenges for the study of vision.

30   Fodor and Pylysyhn try to distance themselves from the usual epistemological debates, claiming that their own arguments are based on empirical premises. I leave it to the reader to decide how far their claims about asymmetries, misperception, the intentionality of vision, etc. stray from more epistemological approaches.

31   Gibson, *Ecological Approach*, p. 166.

32   It goes without saying that even on this narrow account acts of visual recognition or identification that require the application of ordinary concepts or symbols are mentalistically tainted.

33   Gary Hatfield, "Gibsonian Representation and Connectionist Symbol Processing: Prospects for Unitication," Report no. 38/1990, Research Group on Mind and Brain (ZiF), University of Bielefeld. See Hatfield,

"Representation and Content in Some (Actual) Theories of Perception," *Studies in the History and Philosophy of Science*, 19 (1988), pp. 175–214, for more on this issue and related topics. For a somewhat different take on matters, see Vicki Bruce and Patrick Green, *Visual Perception, Physiology, Psychology and Ecololgy* (Lawrence Erlbaum, Hillsdale, N.J., 1985), ch. 14, esp. pp. 326–31.

34   See Paul Smolensky, "On the Proper Treatment of Connectionism," *Behavioral and Brain Sciences*, 11 (1988), pp. 1–74. For more on the controversy, see Steven Pinker and Jacques Mehler (eds), *Connections and Symbols* (MIT Press, Cambridge, Mass., 1988). For some theorists the difference between symbolic and nonsymbolic representation depends on whether the representations are digital or analog. This distinction is itself drawn in many different ways and often does not match up with the non-connectionist – connectionist split.

35   See Jerry Fodor, *A Theory of Content and Other Essays*, (MIT Press, Cambridge, Mass., 1990), esp. pp. 127–31. "A good theory of content might license literal ascription of (underived) intentionality to thermometers, thermostats, and the like. . . . I don't think that should count as a reductio, though (in my view) the ascription of beliefs and desires to thermometers and thermostats certainly would" (p. 130).
      It has also been argued that even on this attenuated version of intentionality, Fodor's approach to representation would rule out various symbolic schemes found in prominent visual theories.

36   See Jacob Beck and James J. Gibson, "The Relation of Apparent Shape to Apparent Slant in the Perception of Objects," *Journal of Experimental Psychology*, 50 (1955), pp. 125–33, for an early statement of these differences.

37   It has been argued that there really is no coherent *de re* sense of perception or of propositional attitude concepts in general. But the relevant considerations on this topic are far removed from issues peculiar to the theory of vision.

38   For a detailed analysis of Berkeley's position here, see Margaret Atherton, "Corpuscles, Mechanism and Essentialism in Berkeley and Locke," *Journal of the History of Philosophy*, 29 (1991), pp. 47–67.

39   See Fred Dretske, *Knowledge and the Flow of Information* (MIT Press, Cambridge, Mass., 1981) and Jerry Fodor, *Psychosemantics* (MIT Press, Cambridge, Mass., 1987), for versions of this approach to the problem of naturalizing semantics. For more on the general issue of signs and symbols, see my entry "Representation," in *Companion to the Philosophy of Mind*, ed. S. Guttenplan (Basil Blackwell, Oxford, forthcoming).

40   See Fodor and Pylyshyn, "How Direct is Perception?," p. 187, where it is noted that representations like David Marr's primal sketch may be entirely stimulus-driven and in one-to-one correspondence with the stimulus.

41   Robert Schwartz, "I'm Going to Make You a Star," *Midwest Studies in Philosophy*, 11 (1986), pp. 427–39.
42   My position has strong affinities with the relativistic approach to ontology that Nelson Goodman has long espoused, as well as with Arthur Fine's more recent natural ontological attitude, NOA.
43   This worry is reiterated in his last book, *Ecological Approach*, p. 223.

Bibliography

Abbott, Thomas, *Sight and Touch: An Attempt to Disprove the Received (or Berkeleian) Theory of Vision*, Longman, Green Longman, Roberts and Green, London, 1964.

Armstrong, D. M., *Berkeley's Theory of Vision*, Melbourne University Press, Melbourne, 1960.

Atherton, Margaret, *Berkeley's Revolution in Vision*, Cornell University Press, Ithaca, N.Y., 1990.

Atherton, Margaret, "Corpuscles, Mechanism and Essentialism in Berkeley and Locke," *Journal of the History of Philosophy*, 29 (1991), pp. 47–67.

Austin, J. L., *Sense and Sensibilia*, Oxford University Press, Oxford, 1964.

Barrow, H. G. and Tenenbaum, J. M., "Computational Approaches to Vision," in *Handbook of Perception and Human Performance*, vol. 2, ed. K. Boff, L. Kaufman and J. Thomas, Wiley, New York, 1986, ch. 38.

Beck, Jacob and Gibson, James J., "The Relation of Apparent Shape to Apparent Slant in the Perception of Objects," *Journal of Experimental Psychology*, 50 (1955), pp. 125–33.

Berkeley, George, *The Works of George Berkeley, Bishop of Cloyne* (9 vols), ed. A. A. Luce and T. E. Jessop, Thomas Nelson, Edinburgh, 1948–57.

Bower, T. G. R., *Development in Infancy*, W. H. Freeman, San Francisco, 1974.

Bruce, Vicki and Green, Patrick, *Visual Perception, Physiology, Psychology and Ecology*, Lawrence Erlbaum, Hillsdale, N.J., 1985.

Carlson, V. R., "Instruction and Perceptual Constancy Judgments," in *Stability and Constancy in Perception: Mechanisms and Processes*, ed. William Epstein, Wiley, New York, 1977, pp. 217–54.

Dennett, Daniel, *Consciousness Explained*, Little Brown, Boston, 1991.

Descartes, René, *Le Monde, ou Traité de la lumière*, tr. Michael Mahoney, Arabis Books, New York, 1979.

Donagan, Alan, "Berkeley's Theory of the Immediate Objects of Vision," in *Studies in Perception*, ed. P. Machamer and R. Turnbull, Ohio State University Press, Columbus, 1978, pp. 312–35.

Dretske, Fred, *Knowledge and the Flow of Information*, MIT Press, Cambridge, Mass., 1981.

Dretske, Fred, *Seeing and Knowing*, University of Chicago Press, Chicago, 1969.

Epstein, W., Park, J. and Casey, A., "The Current Status of the Size–Distance Hypothesis," *Psychological Bulletin*, 58 (1961), pp. 491–514.

Firth, Roderick, "Sense Experience," in *Handbook of Perception*, vol. 1, ed. Edward Carterette and Morton Friedman, Academic Press, New York, 1974, pp. 3–18.

Fodor, Jerry, *Psychosemantics*, MIT Press, Cambridge, Mass., 1987.

Fodor, Jerry, *A Theory of Content and Other Essays*, MIT Press, Cambridge, Mass., 1990.

Fodor, Jerry and Pylyshyn, Zenon, "How Direct is Perception? Some Reflections on Gibson's 'Ecological Approach,'" *Cognition*, 9 (1981), pp. 139–96.

Gibson, James J., *The Ecological Approach to Visual Perception*, Houghton Mifflin, Boston, 1979.

Gibson, James J., *The Perception of the Visual World*, Houghton Mifflin, Boston, 1950.

Gibson, James J., *Reasons for Realism: Selected Essays of James J. Gibson*, ed. Edward Reed and Rebecca Jones, Lawrence Erlbaum, Hillsdale, N.J., 1982.

Gibson, James J., "Three Kinds of Distance that can be Seen, or How Bishop Berkeley Went Wrong," in *Studies in Perception: Festschrift for Fabio Metelli*, ed. G. Flores D'Arcais, Martello-Guinti, Milan and Florence, 1976.

Gibson, J. J. and Gibson, E. J., "Perceptual Learning: Differentiation or Enrichment?," *Psychological Review*, 62 (1955), pp. 32–41.

Gregory, R. L., "Perception as Hypotheses," in *Philosophy of Psychology*, ed. S. C. Brown, Macmillan, London, 1974, pp. 195–210.

Hanson, Norwood R., *Patterns of Discovery*, Cambridge University Press, Cambridge, 1965.

Harman, Gilbert, *Thought*, Princeton University Press, Princeton, N.J., 1973.

Hatfield, Gary, "Gibsonian Representation and Connectionist Symbol-Processing Prospects for Unitication," Report no. 38/1990, Research Group on Mind and Brain (ZiF), University of Bielefeld.

Hatfield, Gary, *The Natural and the normative*, MIT Press, Cambridge, Mass., 1990.

Hatfield, Gary, "Representation and Content in Some (Actual) Theories of Perception," *Studies in the History and Philosophy of Science*, 19 (1988), pp. 175–214.

Hatfield, Gary and Epstein, William, "The Sensory Core and the Medieval Foundations of Early Modern Perceptual Theory," *Isis*, 70 (1979), pp. 363–84.

Held, Richard, "Plasticity in Sensory-Motor Systems," in *Perception: Mechanisms and Models*, ed. Richard Held and Whitman Richards, W. H. Freeman, San Francisco, 1972.

Helmholtz, Hermann von, "The Origin of the Correct Interpretation of our Sensory Impressions," in *Helmholtz on Perception: Its Physiology and Development*, ed. Richard Warren and Roslyn Warren, Wiley, New York, 1968, pp. 249–60.

Helmholtz, Hermann von, "The Recent Progress of the Theory of Vision," in *Helmholtz on Perception: Its Physiology and Development*, ed. Richard Warren and Roslyn Warren, Wiley, New York, 1968, pp. 61–136.

Helmholtz, Hermann von, *Treatise on Physiological Optics* (3 vols), ed. James Southall, Dover, New York, 1950.

Hershenson, Maurice (ed.), *The Moon Illusion*, Lawrence Erlbaum, Hillsdale, N.J., 1989.

Hochberg, Julian, "Higher-Order Stimuli and Inter-Response Coupling in the Perception of the Visual World," in *Perception: Essays in Honor of James J. Gibson*, ed. R. B. Macleod and H. L. Pick, Cornell University Press, Ithaca, N.Y., 1974, pp. 17–39.

Hochberg, Julian, "On Cognition in Perception: Perceptual Coupling and Unconscious Inference," *Cognition*, 10 (1981), pp. 127–34.

Hochberg, Julian, *Perception*, Prentice-Hall, Englewood Cliffs, N.J., 1965.

Hochberg, Julian, "Perception, I and II," in *Woodworth and Schlossberg's Experimental Psychology*, ed. J. Kling and L. Riggs, Holt, Rinehart and Winston, New York, 1971, pp. 395–550.

Hofsten, Claes von, "Binocular Convergence as a Determinant of Reaching Behavior in Children," *Perception*, 6 (1977), pp. 139–44.

Ittelson, W. H., *Visual Space Perception*, Springer, New York, 1960.

James, William, *The Principles of Psychology* (2 vols), Dover, New York, 1950.

Kaufman, Lloyd, *Sight and Mind*, Oxford University Press, Oxford, 1974.

Kaufman, Lloyd, *Perception: The World Transformed*, Oxford University Press, Oxford, 1979.

Kaufman, Lloyd and Rock, Irvin, "The Moon Illusion," *Scientific American*, 207 (1962), pp. 120–31.

Kline, A. David, "Berkeley, Pitcher and Distance Perception," *International Studies in Philosophy*, 12 (1980), pp. 1–8.

Koffka, Kurt, *Principles of Gestalt Psychology*, Harcourt, Brace and World, New York, 1935.

Lindberg, David, *Theories of Vision from Al-Kindy to Kepler*, University of Chicago Press, Chicago, 1976.

Locke, John, *An Essay Concerning Human Understanding*, ed. Peter Nidditch, Clarendon Press, Oxford, 1975.

Marr, David, *Vision*, W. H. Freeman, San Francisco, 1982.

McCready, Don, "On Size, Distance and Visual Angle Perception," *Perception & Psychophysics*, 37 (1985), pp. 323–34.

Mill, John Stuart, "Bailey on Berkeley's Theory of Vision," in *Dissertations and Discussions*, vol. 2, Haskell House Publications, New York, 1973, pp. 84–119.

Natsoulas, Thomas, "'Why Do Things Look As They Do?' Some Gibsonian

Answers to Koffka's Question," *Philosophical Psychology*, 4 (1991), pp. 183–202.

Ono, Hiroshi and Comerford, James, "Stereoscopic Depth Constancy," in *Stability and Constancy in Visual Perception*, ed. William Epstein, Wiley, New York, 1977, pp. 91–128.

Oyama, Tadasu, "Analysis of Causal Relations in the Perceptinal Gustancies," in *Stability and Constancy in Visual Perception*, ed. William Epstein, Wiley, New York, 1977, pp. 183–216.

Pinker, Steven and Mehler, Jacques (eds), *Connections and Symbols*, MIT Press, Cambridge, Mass., 1988.

Pitcher, George, *Berkeley*, Routledge and Kegan Paul, London, 1977.

Reed, Edward, *James J. Gibson and the Psychology of Perception*, Yale University Press, New Haven, Conn., 1988.

Rock, Irvin, *An Introduction to Perception*, Macmillan, New York, 1975.

Rock, Irvin, "Inference in Perception," in *PSA 1992*, vol. 2, ed. P. Asquith and T. Nickles, Philosophy of Science Association, East Lansing, Mich., 1983, pp. 525–40.

Rock, Irvin, *The Logic of Perception*, MIT Press, Cambridge, Mass., 1983.

Rock, Irvin, *The Nature of Perceptual Adaptation*, Basic Books, New York, 1966.

Rorty, Richard, *Philosophy and the Mirror of Nature*, Princeton University Press, Princeton, N.J., 1979.

Russell, Bertrand, *Human Knowledge: Its Scope and Limits*, Simon and Schuster, New York, 1964.

Schwartz, Robert, "I'm Going to Make You a Star," *Midwest Studies in Philosophy*, 11 (1986), pp. 427–39.

Schwartz, Robert, "*The* Problems of Representation," *Social Research*, 51 (1984), pp. 1047–64.

Schwartz, Robert, "Representation," in *Companion to the Philosophy of Mind*, ed. S. Guttenplan, Basil Blackwell, Oxford, forthcoming.

Schwartz, Robert, Review of *Vision*, by David Marr, *Philosophical Review*, 94 (1985), pp. 411–4.

Sedgwick, H. A., "Environment-Centered Representation of Spatial Layout: Available Visual Information from Texture and Perspective," in *Human and Machine Vision*, ed. Jacob Beck, Barbara Hope and Azriel Rosenfeld, Academic Press, New York, 1983, pp. 425–58.

Sedgwick, H. A., "The Geometry of Spatial Layout in Pictorial Representation," in *The Perception of Pictures*, ed. Margaret Hagen, Academic Press, New York, 1980.

Sigman, E. and Rock, I., "Stroboscopic Movement Based on Perceptual Intelligence," *Perception*, 3 (1974), pp. 9–28.

Smolensky, Paul, "On the Proper Treatment of Connectionism," *Behavioral and Brain Sciences*, 11 (1988), pp. 1–74.

Stich, Stephen, "Beliefs and Subdoxastic States," *Philosophy of Science*, 45 (1978), pp. 499–518.

Sully, James, "The Question of Visual Perception in Germany, I & II," *Mind*, 9 (1878), pp. 1–23, 167–95.

Tipton, I. C., *Berkeley: The Philosophy of Immaterialism*, Methuen, London, 1974.

Turbayne, C. M., Editor's Commentary, in *George Berkeley, Works on Vision*, Bobbs-Merrill, Indianapolis, 1963.

Turbayne, C. M., *The Myth of Metaphor*, University of South Carolina Press, Columbia, 1970.

Turvey, M. T., Shaw, R. E., Reed, E. S. and Mace, W. M., "Ecological Laws of Perceiving and Acting: In Reply to Fodor and Pylyshyn (1981)," *Cognition*, 9 (1981), pp. 237–304.

Ullman, Shimon, "Against Direct Perception," *Behavioral and Brain Sciences*, 3 (1980), pp. 373–415.

Ullman, Shimon, *The Interpretation of Visual Motion*, MIT Press, Cambridge, Mass., 1979.

Warnock, G. J., *Berkeley*, Penguin, London, 1953.

Welch, Robert, "Adaptation of Space Perception," in *Handbook of Perception and Human Performance*, vol. 1, ed. K. Boff, L. Kaufman and J. Thomas, Wiley, New York, 1986, ch. 24.

Welch, Robert, *Perceptual Modification: Adapting to Actered Sensory Environments*, Academic Press, New York, 1978.

Wundt, Wilhelm, *Lectures on Human and Animal Psychology*, tr. J. E. Creighton and E. B. Thorndike, Macmillan, New York, 1896.

Yonas, A. and Pick, H. L., "An Approach to the Study of Infant Space Perception," in *Infant Perception: From Sensation to Perception*, vol. 2, ed. L. Cohen and S. Salapatek, Academic Press, New York, 1975, pp. 3–31.

Index

Printed in the United States
803500004B